£1.50
2013

Singapc

GW01606958

A History and Guide

Bonnie Tinsley

TIMES BOOKS International

The Author

The daughter of an avid gardener, Bonnie Tinsley was born in Washington, D.C. and graduated from the College of William and Mary, Williamsburg, Virginia (the oldest institution of higher education in the United States). From the suburbs of Washington by way of the Illinois and Indiana cornbelt, this published poet, translator and art critic came to Singapore in 1981. While freelancing as a features writer for *The Straits Times*, she worked as a volunteer tour guide at the National Museum.

Ms Tinsley received her Masters Degree in English Literature in 1970, and her poetry has been published throughout the midwestern United States. The Illinois Arts Council awarded her a grant for the poetry chapbook *Daddy Never Bought Me A Horse*. As Director of Public Information for the Indiana Committee for the Humanities, she won two design awards for her publications.

Believing that we know ourselves best in our relationship to nature, she has always found her poetry rooted in the world of plants, taking inspiration and images from as stark a setting as the corn and soy bean fields of Illinois, where she lived and worked as a small truck farmer and organic gardener in the early 1970s. More recently, her strengths of research and poetic imagination have found their source in Singapore and its lush tropical vegetation.

© **1983 Times Books International**
Times Centre
1 New Industrial Road
Singapore 1953

All rights reserved. No part of this publication may be reproduced, stored in a retrieval system, or transmitted, in any form or by any means, electronic, mechanical, photocopying, recording or otherwise, without the prior permission of the copyright holder.

Design by Jenny Soh
Illustrations by May Kong

Printed by Khai Wah Press, Singapore

ISBN 9971 65 136 X

For
my mother,
Hawthorne Agner,
and the gifts
from her 'green thumb'

Contents

Acknowledgements

Not being an expert but rather one who fell under the spell of the Botanic Gardens, I had much to learn about tropical plants when I began this project well over a year ago. Fortunately, all along the way of my total immersion programme in the mysterious language of tropical flora, I had the help of experts at the Gardens – mainly Mrs Ng Siew Yin, Assistant Commissioner, whose careful reading and correction of the manuscript kept it on the side of scientific accuracy. I am also indebted to the Curators for information and help generously given: Dr Christopher Hails (Ornithology), Mr J.F. Maxwell (Plant Introduction), and Mr Tay Eng Pin (Maintenance), who gives an exhaustive tour of the Gardens. For day-in-day-out assistance with reference materials and a good deal of fun, I have Librarian Johan Abdul Rahman to thank, and his assistant, Mr Abdul Aziz Ahmad.

To Geraldine Lowe-Ismail, whose walking tour initially sparked my curiosity about folk uses of the plants, to members of the Malayan Nature Society and the SEA Room staff of the National Library for the delight in shared moments of discovery – I am indeed grateful.

Throughout the research and writing, I have used the tools of scholarship. However, since the book is meant for the pleasure of a general readership, I chose not to use formal documentation which becomes ponderous and tends to weigh the reader down. Anyone wishing more specific source information may contact me through Times Books International; in fact, I welcome such requests as the subject of the Gardens and its history is a matter of continuing interest to me.

One final word. Most cities have their shopping sprawls, and so I find nothing special in Singapore's. To my mind, the real riches of Singapore lie first in her people and secondly in her parks. Not to maintain these 'natural resources' – the Botanic Gardens and other parks, the nature reserves, the catchment areas and mangrove swamps – would be the poorer for civilization. They may, in the end, help save our spirits from destruction.

Publishers' Acknowledgements

Most of the photographs in this book were supplied by the author and taken by her husband, Cliff F. Richeson. For the rest, the publishers wish to thank the following: **Singapore Botanic Gardens** for the colour transparencies on orchid culture (p. 82), as well as assistance in obtaining photographs of the Gardens' Superintendents and Directors (pp. 22, 32, 42-4), the 1866 map of the Gardens (p. 23), illustrations of proposed extensions to the Gardens (pp. 54-5, 57), and the De Alwis paintings of Gardens' specimens (pp. 33-6); **Parks and Recreation Division** for permission to reproduce their logo (p. 52); **Royal Botanic Gardens** for the photograph on p. 16 (Crown Copyright, reproduced with the permission of the Controller of Her Majesty's Stationery Office and of the Director, Royal Botanic Gardens, Kew); **Singapore National Archives** for the 1828 plan of Singapore Town (pp. 18-19); **Mr Koh Seow Chuan** for postcards reproduced from his collection (pp. 14, 25, 30, 39, 45, 47 and 53); and **Straits Times Picture Library** for the photographs on pp. 26-7, 48, 50 and 51.

A family outing at the Botanic Gardens, 1949.

Introduction

A TREASURE AMONG the world's great tropical gardens, the Botanic Gardens is one of Singapore's truly irresistible attractions. Rarely can a city as compact as Singapore boast a spacious garden in its very midst – offering visual delight and sanctuary to daily strollers and the most ardent lovers of green. For many years, the Gardens has been the verdant backdrop for family outings, for band concerts and school field trips. Newcomers to Singapore invariably request of cabbies: 'Take me to the Botanic Gardens.' Botanists from every landed edge of the globe have come to study the tropical flora and the vast repository of plant specimens in the Herbarium – all testifying to its importance as a place of recreation, education and research.

As the story of Singapore unfolds, so does that of her oldest national park. Our story begins with Raffles' foundation of a settlement on Singapore Island in 1819 and with it his vision of an experimental spice plot on Government Hill. Through the years of experimentation with and extraordinarily successful introduction of rubber and other useful crops to the region, carried on at the present Tanglin site, until today's orchid industry with its thriving export trade – the work of the Gardens has supplied vital nourishment to the spirit and the economic veins of the Island State.

Firmly planted in Botanic Gardens' soil grew rubber seedlings that stocked the plantations of Southeast Asia and parented the region's early economic prosperity. Henry Nicholas Ridley, Director of the Gardens from 1888 to 1912, earned the title 'father of the Malayan rubber industry' for his foresight and persistent faith in the uses of rubber. 'Mad' Ridley, who advanced on unsuspecting Malayan plantation owners with pockets full of rubber seeds and crusader zeal, stands as the most significant figure after Raffles in Singapore's history. More of Ridleyana later. Here it is sufficient to say that during Ridley's tenure was established the international reputation the Botanic Gardens enjoys today.

Even though the most famous, Ridley takes his place in a long line of administrators, staff and other personalities who contribute to the legend of the Gardens: the intrepid gardener Miss Joaquim, after whom Singapore's national flower is named; Ahmad bin Hassan, more than 60 years with the Gardens and a 'walking dictionary' on Malayan flora; the planter Tan Chay Yan who was the first to take a risk on rubber; distinguished administrators such as E.J.H. Corner and R.E. Holttum, who with their Japanese captors preserved the Gardens from destruction during the turbulent years of World War Two; the Lake's man-eating crocodile, the ill-tempered staff of monkeys, and a host of ghostly luminaries the light of the Gardens cannot catch. Each life a story in itself; each story rooted deep in the making of the Gardens.

Since the early days of horse and carriage promenades, and the pomp and toot of military band performances at the Bandstand, the Gardens has determined its mission in community service. Farmers have looked to the Botanic Gardens for guidance in methods of plant cultivation and control of pests and diseases. Growers, home gardeners and others in the public sector have regularly sought the Gardens' curatorial services in identifying a myriad of plant specimens. And occasionally the police will call on the Gardens to identify plant samples that figure in their criminal investigations.

The breeding and introduction of new orchids and other plant varieties suitable to local conditions has been another important ongoing activity. In fact, until the 1970s the Gardens' professional supervision and much of its stock was largely responsible for the beauty of Singapore's landscape, the luxuriance of trees and flowering shrubs that gave the Island its reputation of 'Clean and Green'. This responsibility is now under the jurisdiction of the Parks and Recreation Department officers.

For over 50 years the Gardens has concentrated on orchid breeding with impressive results to support its international acclaim as one of the world's pioneers in the production of orchid hybrids. From far and wide, visitors have come to admire the Gardens' orchid collection and the flower that has become a symbol of Singapore. Thus it is not surprising that when foreign heads of state arrive in the Republic, the diplomatic welcome frequently includes a visit to the Orchid Enclosure. There one of the new hybridized orchids is presented to and named after the visiting 'first lady' – orchids such as those now graced with the names of *Dendrobium* Tsutako Nakasone, *Doritaenopsis* Elizabeth Waldheim, and *Aranda* Imelda Romualdez Marcos.

Today the Gardens holds a living museum where plants of scientific value are nurtured and exhibited for the study and pleasure of the expert and non-expert alike. Carefully identified by taxonomic classification and place of origin, majestic palms, sprawling fig trees, indigenous and exotic ornamental and economic plants rise from the soil as surely as the seasons. In keeping with today's nature conservation campaign, the Gardens takes measures to conserve its endangered species and its small tract of native jungle. Indigenous trees are re-planted, and the resources of vanishing orchid species are being preserved through a programme of self-pollination.

While preserving the past, the Gardens also devotes considerable time to tropical plant research and international resource exchange, concentrating efforts in the areas of hybrid propagation and horticultural experimentation. The School of Ornamental Horticulture, founded in 1972, offers diploma and certificate courses encompassing the full range of horticultural studies. Graduates trained as horticultural assistants apply their ornamental art to the Island's perennial bloom.

Through the week we may see the dogged beat of joggers along the winding roads, wedding parties in a flurry of white posing against an orchid rainbow, or, in a more quiet mood, senior citizens practising the graceful Chinese art of taiji. Just past the Main Gate and to the left, the Traveller's Palm (*Ravenala madagascariensis*) opens enormous fans to the sky. In its native Madagascar, it provides a constant source of rain water just by cutting the lower portion of the leaf-stalks. This distinctive palm-like plant related to the banana is one of some 80 per cent of the Gardens' plants which have been acquired through foreign exchange or collecting expeditions.

Further along the road and uphill to the right on Lawn E, an old guardian, the magnificent Tembusu (*Fagraea fragrans*) seems to spread like an umbrella over all the Gardens. The hard-boned timber of the native Tembusu has been the durable stuff of chopping blocks and ancient Muslim grave posts.

From the calm surface of the Lake, to the soft music of the Miniature Waterfall, to the four hectares of virgin forest, the Orchid Enclosure, Palm Valley and beyond – a walk through the Singapore Botanic Gardens is a two-hour excursion into the mysteries of a green pleasure dome.

But before we have our stroll through the Gardens, let us turn back the leaves of time to 1819 and, with Raffles and his crew, peer through the mangrove thicket onto an island hillside, soon to bear the tender beginnings of a spice garden . . .

A History of the Botanic Gardens in Singapore From 1819

From Spice Plot to Pleasure Garden

On 28 January 1819 the stout vessel *Indiana* and her escorts passed through the Straits of Malacca and dropped anchor just off the ancient port called Singapura. On board, Raffles swept his telescope across marshy swamp and thick scrub, broken by the sharp angles of attap huts. He could make out empty patches of a hillside beyond the shore, and then dense jungle blocked all but the sky.

Next morning, satisfied of its friendliness, Raffles and his retinue made their way by canoe through a circuitous waterway of mangrove to the village and its Malay chief. Once they had cut their way through the mangrove thicket, the river eased into open swamp and now and then clusters of towering coconut palm. According to Raffles' guide, Abdullah bin Abdul Kadir, who kept a diary of the expedition, the riverside district they found was thick with scrub, but in the open spaces, Myrtle, Rhododendron and *Eugenia* trees cast their branching shadows.

Sarong-clad villagers decorously served the new arrivals a tropical feast of locally-grown fruit. Out of baskets made of woven banana leaf tumbled starfruit, miniature bananas and other sweet mysteries. In addition to fishing and the manly art of piracy, these people made their living by gathering the natural fruits of jungle trees. Up in the hill country, Chinese cultivators were methodically clearing the jungle for their gambier plantations – and waiting for the annual northeast monsoon that brought rice and other supplies in exchange for their product. Already the stage was set for Singapore's future prosperity by sea *and* land.

As soon as the ritual formalities of the treaty with the Temenggong were accomplished, Raffles set about discovering the natural virtues of his infant settlement. One of his first duties was to assign the task of gathering samples of the local flora and fauna. In addition to all manner of wriggling worms and insects, men returned from the jungle with leaves, flowers, fungi, mosses and so on, which Raffles pressed between the thick pages of a book. An expert Chinese draftsman from Macau on his staff made careful copies of the more perishable fruits and flowers.

With the construction of Raffles' bungalow, an experimental garden was laid out on the slopes of Government Hill. Towards the close of 1819 Raffles sent a gardener named Dunn to plant clove and nutmeg trees in his garden. These 125 trees and 1000 seeds of nutmeg, and 450 clove plants, formed the foundation of Singapore's flourishing spice plantations which dominated the Island landscape for the next 35 years.

Interest in things botanical had a twofold purpose during the centuries of global exploration and colonization. Naturalists attached to these voyages of discovery, colonial officials, and

The Palm House at the Royal Botanic Gardens, Kew around 1850.

travellers collected specimens of exotic flora to carry back home for study. Home governments also encouraged the foundation of experimental gardens devoted to useful or revenue-earning crops, research and preservation of native plants.

Thus Singapore fell heir to the long-established custom of developing European botanical gardens in the tropics, with such noteworthy forerunners as Pamplemousse in Mauritius, and the botanical gardens of Calcutta, Trinidad, Penang, Bogor in Java, and Sri Lanka's Peradeniya. The Royal Botanic Gardens at Kew, founded in 1759 near the river Thames, became pre-eminent among the seats of plant learning and was responsible for much of the inspiration and administration of these new ventures.

Under the influence of Kew Gardens' Director, Sir Joseph Banks, and the scientific circle of the Royal Society, Raffles had decided to apply himself directly to the study of natural history and actively sought out those who might further this interest. Up until the time of his death in 1820, Banks advised

Raffles and Raffles sent botanical and zoological specimens to Banks – much to the displeasure of the East India Company at spending company funds in this manner!

Raffles' first instructor in botanical subjects was the English naturalist and his good friend, Dr Joseph Arnold. During a collecting trip in Sumatra, it was actually Arnold, rather than Raffles, who first discovered that five-petalled, red and mottled malodorous wonder, *Rafflesia Arnoldi*, which bears the world's largest flower.

It was the friendship between Raffles and Dr Nathaniel Wallich, however, that sealed the fate of the first botanic gardens in Singapore. A widely respected Danish surgeon and naturalist who was then serving as Superintendent of the Royal Gardens at Calcutta, Wallich had occasion to visit Singapore during October and November 1822. He stayed longer than intended in an effort to recover his health. Passing many long and sociable hours in his company, Raffles came to ask for and rely on Wallich's advice on various public affairs of the rapidly growing town. And together they devised a much grander scheme for the tender spice plot.

With Raffles' encouragement, Wallich wrote a glowing report destined to sway the seat of government toward the quick establishment of a botanic and experimental garden on the Island. In a letter to Raffles dated 2 November 1822, Wallich describes Singapore as being

> under circumstances the most favourable for indigenous as well as foreign vegetation and forming part of the richest archipelago in the world – its soil yielding to none in fertility, its climate not exceeded by any in uniformity, mildness and salubrity. It abounds in an endless variety of plants equally interesting to the botanist, the agriculturist and the gardener, with unrivalled facilities and opportunities of disseminating these treasures and exchanging them for others.

Wallich went on calling attention to the Island's rare plants

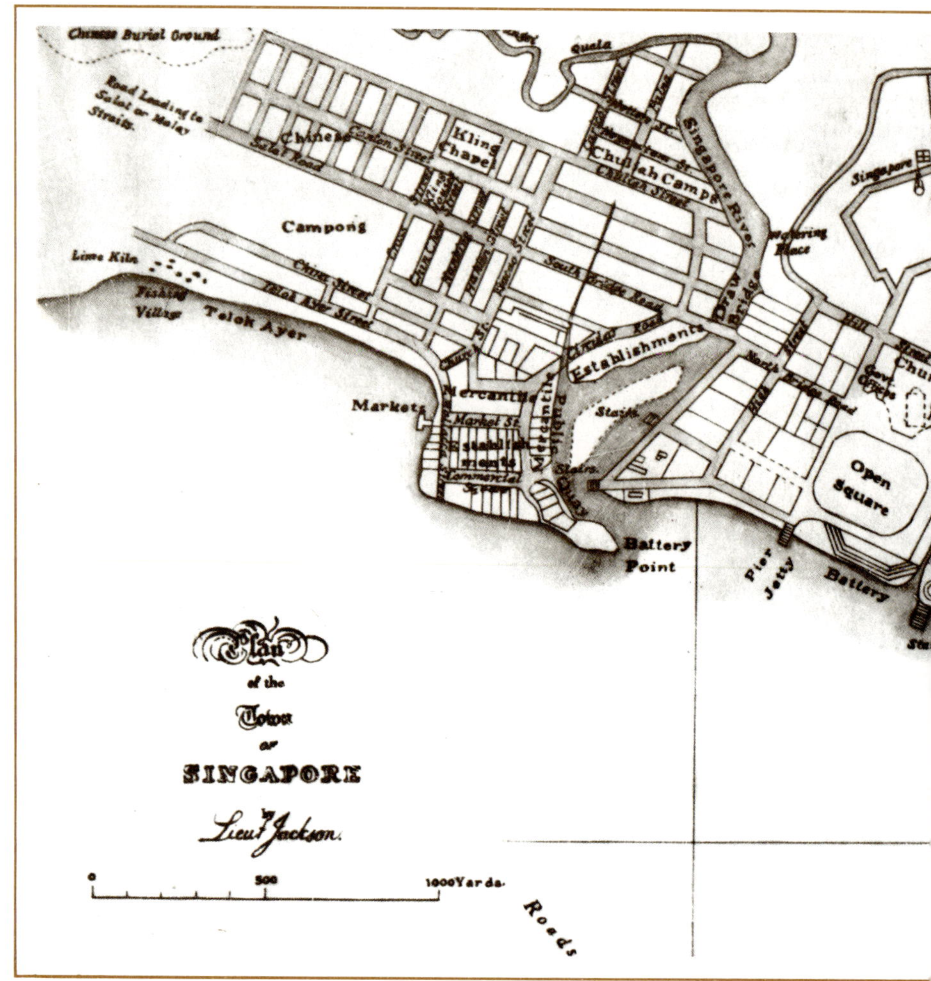

Plan of Singapore Town which shows the site of the Experimental Gardens.

unknown to European collectors, the primeval forests that would surely yield timber fit for ship and house, and the great success already proven in the cultivation of clove, nutmeg, pepper, gambier, sugarcane, coffee and tea. Given the Island's receptive terrain, nothing would stand in the way of reaping these bountiful natural riches – not mountains, ravines or ferocious animals!

The proposed 19-hectare site would take in the current government garden and form an oblong tract. A park ornamented with trees and shrubs would be laid out and Assistant Surgeon William Montgomerie would take charge. Support and services of ten labourers and an overseer would be covered by $60, plus the splendid donation of $1000 by its munificent founder and first patron, Sir Stamford Raffles.

Permission from the supreme authority at Bengal was slow in coming. The correspondence between Raffles and Wallich grew warm and more intimate as Raffles sounded out these and other frustrations with the trading station – mainly with enemies who wished to undermine his administration. Nevertheless, as was his way in the face of opposition, Raffles forged ahead, cutting walks and constructing fencing to protect the young trees, as he was determined 'to lay out both the Garden & Hill before I quit the place,' he says in a letter dated 5 January 1823.

During this time, Raffles suffered unspeakable hardships. In his letters to Wallich, he reports being constantly beseiged by migraine headache attacks. His complete store of natural history records and specimens from Singapore went up in smoke with the carrier ship *Fame*. And he lost to death many close associates, and finally his child, Flora. But his ongoing faith in the colony and the dreams both men shared of a botanic gardens in Singapore gave heart to these letters, like small cloud clearings in the midst of raging storm.

In June 1823, at the end of Raffles' last term of residence in Singapore, Dr Montgomerie was left in charge of the gardens. Since Montgomerie's primary responsibility was medical support for the settlement and his time to the gardens gratuitous, he gave attention solely to the already thriving spices.

To maintain the roads, railings, 6-metre terraces, some 200 nutmeg trees in the nursery and sadly barren clove trees required expenditure which the East India Company would not cover. Thus, in June 1829, Singapore's first Botanic Gardens was discontinued and subsequently parcelled out – to the Armenians for a church, to the Reverend Darrah for a school, and for the construction of a hospital – the site which today takes in the National Museum and the National Library.

In the meantime, the Island's agriculture was growing by leaps and bounds. Ventures in cotton, coffee, cinnamon, cocoa and indigo proved unsuccessful; however, soil and climate were admirably suited to growing coconut, durian, pineapple and other fruits and vegetables, and especially black pepper and gambier.

These growing agricultural concerns revived interest in the abandoned gardens on Government Hill. In 1836, several planters, the Governor, and local officials formed an Agri-Horticultural Society chaired by Dr Montgomerie. They were given 2.8 hectares of the original 19 which they turned to horticultural care. Costs of upkeep were met by a membership subscription of S$8 annually and through the sale of nutmegs. By 1846 interest had declined and the land reverted back to the government.

Then again in 1859 a group of public-spirited citizens formed a new Agri-Horticultural Society, exchanging the dismal garden remains on Fort Canning for a more promising 23-hectare tract at Tanglin. *The Straits Times* of 12 November 1859 heralded this renewed enterprise with the following:

> We understand some of our enterprising citizens have resolved to establish a Floricultural and Horticultural Society, which will receive our hearty concurrence and support. This will be the third attempt to organise a really useful association, and we trust it will succeed.

The land in question belonged to Hoo Ah Kay, better known by his trade name 'Whampoa', an influential businessman, staunch supporter of the colony, and a key figure in organising the new Singapore Agri-Horticultural Society. Shaped like a tilting bottle, the tract of land was bounded on the north and east by what is today Cluny Road, on the south by Napier Road, and on the west by Tyersall and Dalvey Gate Roads. It was largely undeveloped but rapidly appreciating in value as property in the Tanglin district was becoming fashionable for country houses.

Described as 'a haunt of tigers', the southern portion had once been under cultivation, probably of gambier, and had

reverted to *belukar*. The section at the bottle's neck bore virgin rain forest, 4 hectares of which persist to this day.

Perhaps hopeful of spreading their influence by sheer number, the rather large Society's committee of 14, chaired by the Governor, won 77 subscribers and $1900 in capital. Once financially firm, they set as their main objective the creation of a pleasure garden. They enlisted the services of Lawrence Niven, a planter who supervised an adjoining nutmeg plantation.

By 1861 a regimental band was playing atop the Bandstand Hill, which Niven had terraced and laid out with flower beds

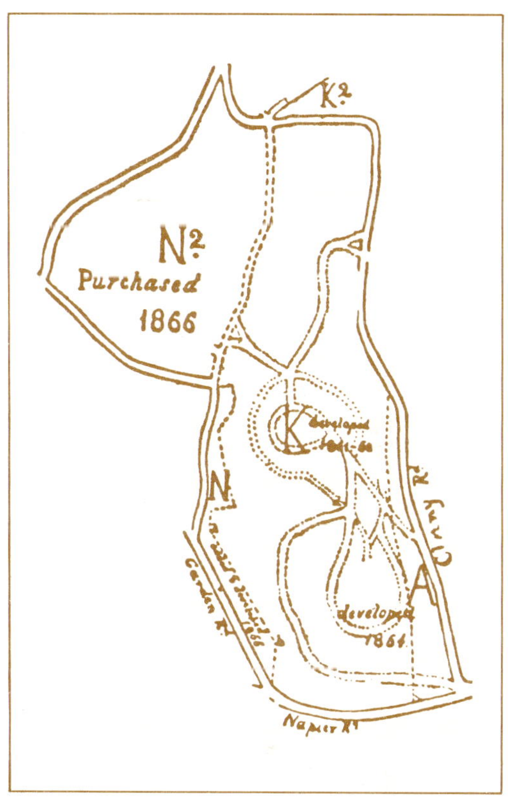

Map of the Botanic Gardens as it was in 1866, showing the original properties and development beginning 1860. (From *Gardens Bulletin*, Vol. II.)

Left: Lawrence Niven, Superintendent 1860–75.

and stands. The first roads curved round the hill, offering evening promenaders an alternative to the Esplanade.

The Gardens' layout grew in four stages beginning with the Bandstand and promenade entering at Cluny Road and exiting at Dalvey Gate Road. Next came the carefully planned Ring Roads and their connecting paths. The Main Gate and its road developed in stage three, followed by the acquisition of a thin strip of land along today's Tyersall Road that was partly excavated for the Lake in 1866. Virtually all of the layout remains today just as it was designed 120 years ago.

The Society organized flower shows to encourage local cultivation and employed two Chinese gardeners to grow vegetables and develop a stock of seeds. But their main thrust was decorative development of the park, and to that end they applied the funds earned from subscriptions and regular 'horticultural fetes and fancy fairs' supervised by the lady members.

In March 1866 the Society purchased an additional 10 hectares to the northwest from the old Napier estate. This was to be the site of a house for the Superintendent. Unfortunately, these worthy goals far exceeded the Society's budget and for the next seven years they were forced to resort to mortgages, grants, and other forms of assistance from the government.

At one point the Governor, Sir Harry Ord, noticing a fall-off in subscribers, suggested that the Gardens might attract more visitors by exhibiting living economic plants and by adding a zoo. Although the Society failed to introduce economic plants, they kept their promise to add a zoo which met with enthusiastic response from local and foreign visitors.

In 1874 the Society's debts had become unmanageable, and they resolved to hand over maintenance of the Gardens to the government, following similar resolutions made months earlier by subscribers to the Raffles Library and Museum. Thus the Gardens fell under the jurisdiction of a strong government-appointed committee that undertook the business of serious reorganization.

Superintendents from Kew

By 1875 the Gardens in Singapore had grown from Raffles' experimental spice plot on Fort Canning Hill to a delightfully landscaped ornamental garden and pleasure park at Tanglin Road – in dire need of a qualified superintendent with a strong background in botany. On the recommendation of Sir Joseph Hooker, the Director of the Royal Gardens at Kew, the government search committee invited Henry James Murton, the first of many Kew-trained men who devoted years of professional and personal service to the Gardens.

Murton was a young man, but a skilled and avid horti-

James Murton, Superintendent 1875–80, with his staff of gardeners (1877 photo).

culturist. His early annual reports reflect an obvious impatience with abusers of the Gardens.

'It is my unpleasant duty,' he says, 'to report many serious infringements of the Rules, not only by natives but also by Europeans. The latter on more than one occasion have been detected cutting flowers by moonlight.' And again he urges that the practice of supplying 700 baskets of flowers to subscribers be modified, if not eliminated altogether, 'as the Gardens can never present a gay appearance under existing circumstances'.

Overall, Murton's reports read like the hurried task of an overworked and understaffed administrator, who would prefer

pure research to clean-up work on the Gardens' grounds. But to Murton's energies goes the credit for altering the character of the Gardens beyond merely a recreational spot to a place of study and serious scientific experimentation.

Murton set up the system of plant exchange with other botanical institutions worldwide and travelled widely and frequently in the Malay Peninsula, thereby adding a great many new and exotic species to the Gardens' collections. He introduced a herbarium, investigated the potential of many economic plants, and was a major force in establishing the Economic Gardens in 1879. This was the 41 hectare site north of the Botanic

BYE-LAWS

1. The Botanical Gardens shall be open to the public daily from sunrise to sunset, and, on nights when the Band plays, to 11 p.m.

2. Carriages of all kinds are admitted, but it is forbidden to feed the horses in the Gardens. A halt can only be made at the side of the walks and where sufficient room can be left for other carriages to pass. No gharries or jinrickshas are allowed to ply for hire in the gardens.

3. Driving or riding over the lawns is strictly prohibited.

4. Walking or playing over the flower beds is prohibited.

5. It is forbidden to touch the plants or flowers, and cutting or removal from the Gardens of any plant, flower, or seed, or anything appertaining to the Gardens, will render those so doing liable to expulsion and prosecution.

6. Fishing or bathing in the lake is prohibited.

7. Dogs are not admitted, unless led by a short string or chain.

8. It is forbidden to enter or leave the Gardens except by the proper entrances and exits.

9. All animals found straying in the Gardens will be impounded or destroyed.

10. Shooting in the Gardens is prohibited.

January, 1889.

From *Guide to Botanic Gardens.*

Gardens which became the experimental station for cultivation of a wide range of economic crops, including the famous *Hevea brasiliensis*, better known as 'rubber'.

Contrary to popular belief, the first live rubber seedlings that reached Singapore were not contraband smuggled out of Brazil. In 1876 some 70,000 seeds from the central valley of the Amazon were shipped to Kew Gardens with the goodwill and cooperation of the Brazilian government. Of the small percentage that germinated at Kew, 22 seedlings in Wardian cases (miniature greenhouses) reached Singapore in good condition in June 1877.

Murton sent 9 to the gardens at Perak, probably 2 to Durian Sabatang near Malacca, and then planted and worried over the remaining 11 in his brood. His report of 1879 tells of his concern over the slow propagation rate of the maturing trees. Even so, most of the rubber in Malaya has come from this original introduction.

For reasons that still are not clear, Murton was dismissed in 1880. His replacement, Nathaniel Cantley, another Kew-trained horticulturist, arrived on the job the same year, fresh from a term as Assistant Superintendent of the Mauritius Gardens. Full of administrative zeal, his detailed and immaculately organized reports tend to overshadow the contributions of his predecessor.

It was Cantley who put the Gardens on a firm systematic footing. Determined to bring order to a rapidly greening enterprise, he hired the staff necessary to the full functioning of the Gardens, carefully labelled plants and trees, and kept everyone informed with voluminous reports. He surveyed and established the first forest reserves and introduced Malayan timber trees in the Economic Gardens. Most of the formal tree planting around the city was due to Cantley's initiation and supervision. Under his department, the ornamental design and planting of 1000 trees and shrubs in the Chinese district was officially opened as 'People's Park' in 1888 – the year of his death.

Rubber Plantation, Singapore.

'Mad' Ridley and the Malayan Rubber Industry

It is fair to say that the history of Singapore's Botanic Gardens is in many respects the history of its dedicated administrators. In this pantheon of celebrated figures, one seems to stand out larger than life: Henry Nicholas Ridley, 'the father of Malaya's rubber industry', and the man second only to Raffles in Singapore's historical 'Who's Who'. From the botany staff of London's Natural History Museum, Ridley came to the Gardens as Director in 1888 and for the next 23 years worked tirelessly to usher the Gardens into the twentieth century and its most productive period historically.

Dubbed 'Mad Ridley', 'Rubber Ridley', and similarly less than flattering names, this tremendously energetic man was responsible for the foundation of Malaya's thriving rubber industry and for the early establishment of the Gardens' international reputation. In the face of official disapproval and no little ridicule, he took the risk of investing his own efforts and the Gardens' resources in planting and tapping the strange little rubber producer from Brazil – the Para rubber tree (*Hevea brasiliensis*).

Based on considerable research in its commercial possibilities, his suggestion to the government to plant rubber on a large scale met with stubborn opposition. Nevertheless, he doggedly pursued his course and eventually drew international attention to the Gardens through a prodigious number of publications devoted to his investigations on rubber and other 'economics'.

Ridley was as angular and irksome a presence as Don Quixote, campaigning with the forcefulness of his own eccentric vision, or so the successful Malayan coffee planters must have thought when he approached them. Armed with pockets full of seeds and a faith in the future of rubber, Ridley went about the region urging everyone to give the new crop a trial.

There was a method in his madness – a method he devised of tapping the rubber trees, called the 'herring-bone', which remains fundamentally unchanged to this day. Conducting experiments on the Gardens' healthy crop, he discovered that by excising and paring the bark, the initial cut to the tree could be reopened at regular intervals, yielding more and better latex without permanent harm to the tree. Then he demonstrated ways of preparing sheets of coagulated latex for market and convinced a few reluctant planters to speculate on this most practical crop.

Among the first to catch Ridley's vision was Tan Chay Yan, a tapioca planter in Malacca who gave 16 hectares of his estate to the planting of Para rubber seeds supplied by Ridley from

Henry Nicholas Ridley, Director 1888–1912. The photo at right shows him with one of his staff and an original trial Para rubber tree in the Economic Gardens.

Saraca cauliflora Taipingensis

On this and the next three pages are turn-of-the-century paintings of the Gardens' botanical specimens by the gifted Ceylonese artist Charles de Alwis, who was attached to the Gardens from 1900 to 1908 during Ridley's tenure. Prized both for accuracy and fine execution, these plant portraits form part of the Herbarium's rare collection.

Eugenia species

Shorea macroptera

Bauhinia integrifolia

the Singapore Botanic Gardens in 1896. By 1901 Tan had devoted some 1200 hectares to rubber, earning him the distinction of being the 'first practical rubber planter in Malaya'. A half century later, the prize-winning orchid hybrid, *Vanda* Tan Chay Yan, was named after the enterprising planter.

Unfortunately for those who had turned a deaf ear to Ridley, the dominant coffee industry on which they had relied peaked in 1897 and then collapsed altogether in the face of Brazilian competition and spreading disease. In desperation, the coffee planters turned to rubber, just in time to answer the demand from the motorcar industry, whose growth was rapidly accelerating as a result of Henry Ford's mass production lines.

Ridley was right, as matters turned out. Para rubber was perfect for Malaya – hardy, comparatively disease resistant, quick to give returns for a nominal investment, and not fussy about where it was planted. On slopes, plains, vacant lots and overworked land, most places could be home to the tough little seed. Ridley had turned the Gardens' forest clearings and waste ground – whatever land was available – to rubber, so that the Gardens was the major source of seed supply when the rubber rush came at turn of century. Records show that by 1917 the Gardens had distributed over 7 million seeds, and Ridley boasted of requests for as many as one million seeds per day.

The Gardens' revenue was greatly multiplied, and Singapore became the major market for trade in rubber. By 1920 Malaya was producing over half the world's rubber, a source of continuing prosperity to the Asean countries – thanks to Ridley and the Botanic Gardens.

Apart from his pioneering role in Malayan rubber, Ridley expanded the Gardens' work in economic botany by encouraging the introduction of other profitable plantation crops from the Americas, such as cocoa and oil palm. He was always eager to promote a good and profitable thing when he saw it.

Seldom do we remember that Ridley was also quite a fancier

of and something of an expert on orchids. In fact, it was during his administration that the orchid hybrid which is today Singapore's national flower was discovered growing in a clump of bamboo in Agnes Joaquim's garden. So thrilled was Miss Joaquim at her beautiful discovery that she rushed straight away to Ridley with the evidence. He confirmed her belief that indeed she had a unique and wonderful plant – a new orchid hybrid unknown to science that flowered year round and multiplied offshoots in all directions. In the *Gardener's Chronicle* of 24 June 1893, Ridley made the formal announcement of this natural hybrid between *Vanda hookerana* and *Vanda teres.* Within a few years the Gardens was distributing *Vanda* Miss Joaquim to growers all over Singapore and Malaya where it quickly became an established favourite. Once again, Ridley knew a good thing . . .

As a field botanist, Ridley explored much of the Peninsula and the Indonesian Archipelago, collecting and describing thousands of hitherto unknown specimens, mainly of higher plants and ferns, which significantly increased the Herbarium collection. In his *Agricultural Bulletin*, the first of the Gardens' serials, he published information on useful local plants such as timbers, rattans, fibres, and drug and dye plants. He prepared over 500 scientific papers and books and a still standard work on *Spices* (1912). After retirement from the Gardens, he completed a five-volume *Flora of the Malay Peninsula* (1922–25) and *The Dispersal of Plants throughout the World* (1930).

When Ridley reached the age of 100 in December 1955, his birthday was celebrated in both Singapore and England with all the lavish attention and accolades befitting the legendary figure he was. Beyond his reputation as a practical scientist and spirited Gardens administrator, the unusual qualities of the man himself had captured the imagination of people everywhere. 'It is a great delight for me,' he wrote, 'to have lived to see Malaya so prosperous, and the Gardens the best Tropical Gardens in the World.'

Economics to Orchids: the Specialist Years

As former adviser on economic botany to the Bengal government, Isaac Henry Burkill (1912–25) seemed an eminently suitable replacement for Ridley. Despite the intervening World War, during his tenure he maintained Ridley's work on plants of economic value and travelled widely throughout the region, accumulating a formidable amount of data on the native uses and behaviour of tropical plants. The culmination of this research was Burkill's monumental *Dictionary of the Economic Products of the Malay Peninsula* (1935). Still the most comprehensive text on the subject, it was reprinted in a two-volume set in 1968.

Work on 'economics' was ultimately discontinued when the

Economic Gardens was given over to the construction of a campus for Raffles College in 1924. The Gardens then shifted its perspective toward native plant ecology, taxonomic botany and horticulture. The paths ahead lay open to individual exploration, and the professional staff took advantage of the Gardens' resources to perform in-depth research and develop specializations.

Thus Burkill specialized in *Dioscorea* (yams), cultivated plants, native medicines and ethnobotany. Assistant Director T.F. Chipp explored *Cryptogams* (fungi), and Chipp's replacement, R.E. Holttum, began a life-long study of ferns with his appointment in 1922. Joining the staff in 1923, C.X. Furtado studied palms, aroids and groups of monocotyledons.

Between 1924 and 1926, the Gardens' Herbarium was expanded with the addition of the Perak Museum collection, and with it came the experienced curator M.R. Henderson. Henderson specialized in the limestone flora of Malaya, Myrtaceae (the Myrtle family), and *Calophyllum* (a genus of the Mangosteen family). In an effort to publicize these diverse botanical studies undertaken by the Gardens' personnel, Burkill replaced Ridley's *Agricultural Bulletin* with the important *Gardens Bulletin, Straits Settlements.*

When Holttum assumed directorship of the Gardens in 1926, he set himself the task of improving its appearance. Attentive to the public's enthusiasm for gardening, he helped form both the Gardening Society and the Orchid Society, introduced many new tropical cultivated plants, and generally improved the Gardens' horticultural practice.

Most significantly during Holttum's term (1926–49), a programme of hybridizing was begun, particularly with orchids. In the Gardens' laboratories, he set up the apparatus based on Knudson's method of growing seedlings in flasks of sterile culture. After much experimentation, the resultant free-flowering orchid hybrids stimulated a thriving orchid nursery industry, and Singapore's orchid export trade was born.

To his ambitious study of ferns and orchids, Holttum added work on bamboos, gingers and other monocotyledons. He was the University of Malaya's first Professor of Botany (1949–54), wrote the classic *Gardening in the Lowlands of Malaya* (1953), and in retirement at Kew Gardens completed the first in his series on the *Revised Flora of Malaya* (1953–). Today he is respected as one of the world's leading botanists and still diligently pursuing the botanical research and writing on tropical flora he began nearly 60 years ago in Singapore.

Professor Holttum's assistant, the gifted botanist E.J.H. Corner, joined the Gardens' staff in 1929. Specializing in fungi, ecology and trees with emphasis on the genus *Ficus* (figs), Corner is probably most remembered for a remarkable innovation in the science of plant collection and field botany. Fascinated by seeing monkeys collecting coconuts along the roadside, he enlisted a troop of berok or pig-tailed monkeys (*Macacus nemestrina*) to collect twigs, flowers, fruits and epiphytes from the humanly inaccessible reaches of tall forest trees. With the assistance of a skilled Malay monkey-trainer, he would instruct the monkeys to retrieve plant material at the tree-tops by pointing out similar fruit and flower examples on the ground.

Corner received some temporarily incapacitating bites from these 'first apes to enter Government Service'. Other cases of monkey bite were reported after a fair-sized population of long-tailed macaques took up residence in the Gardens' jungle. Although regular visitors to the *mau lau* or 'Monkey' Gardens (as it became known among the local Cantonese) enjoyed feeding the monkeys special treats of bananas and peanuts from their cars, the monkeys took a special liking to the newly-planted sapling trees and began foraging around the housing and University district. The problem persisted through the 1960s and, mainly in the interest of maintaining a high standard of horticulture, the Gardens had to take measures to remove the monkeys.

Corner's *Wayside Trees of Malaya* (1940, 1952), *The Life of*

Richard Eric Holttum
Director 1925–49
(Photo taken about 1948)

Isaac Henry Burkill
Director 1912–25
(Photo taken in 1959)

Kwan Koriba
Director 1942–46
(Photo taken in 1957)

Right: J.W. Purseglove
Director 1954–57 (Photo taken in 1971).

Below: Murray Ross Henderson
Director 1949–54 (Photo taken in 1955)

Humphrey Morrison Burkill
Director 1957–69
(Photo taken about 1969)

Arthur George Alphonso
Acting Director 1970–76
(Photo taken in 1982)

Plants (1964), and his *Natural History of Palms* (1966) remain valuable handbooks; however, perhaps his principal contribution to the Gardens and its store of tropical plant knowledge came to light only recently with the publication of *The Marquis* (1981). Ostensibly a biography of Yoshichika Tokugawa who served as President of the Museum and Botanic Gardens from 1942 to 1944, the book details in memoir form Corner's and his colleagues' courageous efforts to preserve the Botanic Gardens and its irreplaceable research properties during the turbulent years of Japanese occupation of Singapore.

E.J.H. Corner, Assistant Director 1929–45
(Photo taken in 1972)

The Japanese Occupation

Directly following the surrender of Singapore, Corner boldly presented himself to the Japanese authorities, fearing the whole progress of science in the Malay Peninsula would be doomed unless immediate action were taken. With a note from the Governor, Sir Shenton Thomas, he requested permission to preserve the scientific collections, libraries and matters of historic importance, particularly at the Botanic Gardens and the Museum. The request was granted.

Then in the midst of a war-torn city, with the possibility of looting and pillage lurking round every corner, Professor Hidezo Tanakadate, Quan Ah Gun, the Gardens' chief clerk, and Corner returned to the Gardens to find trenches dug in the lawns. Shell holes, splintered branches, vast quantities of military weaponry and refuse littered the grounds. The Director's house had been shelled, leaving fractured ceilings and a hole in one corner near the roof.

After nearly a month's reparation work on house and grounds, the Gardens managed to collect itself, shake off the dust of war, and regain its calm centre of research activity. Holttum, Corner and Chief Botanist Furtado were retained to work in the Gardens. The business of administration and maintenance carried on with relatively little interruption under the expertise of two Japanese men of science, Professors Hidezo Tanakadate of Tohoku University and Kwan Koriba of the University of Kyoto. Both Library and Herbarium remained intact, and no further loss to the Gardens was suffered due to the friendship forged between Gardens' and Japanese staff in the common cause of conservation.

Holttum and Corner resumed their collecting expeditions and returned to revision and preparation of professional papers – blessedly rescued from the wild spree of looting that infected the city. And Kwan Koriba immersed himself in research on the growing habits of selected Malayan trees.

Not so fortunate were the careers of 49 members of the outdoor staff who were sent to work on the Siam-Burma Railway – among them J.C. Nauen, a gifted horticulturist and Assistant Curator of the Singapore Botanic Gardens from 1935 to 1939. With Professor Holttum, Nauen helped found the Gardening Society and was a leading force in organizing the Society's flower shows. As Sergeant in the Penang Volunteer Force, Nauen was taken prisoner and, with 22 of his fellow Gardens' workers, lost his life on the infamous Railway.

Post-war Years Through Independence: More Pioneer Work

At first the post-war years were fraught with difficulties – mainly in shortage of staff and in severely limited botanical exploration due to terrorist activity in the Federation of Malaya. In the years following, however, under the able guidance of M.R. Henderson (1949–54) and J.W. Purseglove (1954–57), the full complement of staff was re-established, using local talent to fill appointments in both botanical and horticultural sections.

Ahmad bin Hassan, the pioneer plant collector and a 'walking dictionary' on Malaysian flora, was called out of retirement in 1948 after already having served the Gardens for 40 years. His special talents were once again in demand. With no formal

Ridley and his collector Ahmad bin Hassan, who served the Gardens for 60 years – in the Gardens' jungle, 1909.

training in botany, but tremendous experience in collecting with Ridley and a long line of senior curators, Ahmad knew the exact location of certain species in the Malayan jungle. What was more, he could identify each plant in the Botanic Gardens by sight and smell and knew the age of many. Through a total of 60 years' work with the Gardens and first-hand observation, he had compiled a hand-written dictionary on Malaysian flora and their medicinal value, giving English, Malay and Latin plant names, with illustrations of his sketches and preserved specimens. Plant and Seed Collector, Chief Recorder, Store Keeper and Head Librarian, Ahmad was awarded the British Empire Medal and the Pingat Bakti Setia medal. Like his famous mentor, he lived to be 100.

The new officers were sent overseas for training, and a scheme was devised in cooperation with the University of Malaya to attract botanical researchers to Singapore and stimulate more interest in tropical botany. Plant collecting in Malaya and Borneo resumed. Holttum and Corner's war years' research was published, bringing renewed attention to the important work of the Gardens. Corner returned to the University of Cambridge in 1949 and as Lecturer in Systematic Botany inspired a host of scholarly pilgrimages to the Malayan region. He retired from Cambridge in 1973 as Emeritus Professor of Tropical Botany.

The second generation of Burkills took charge of the Gardens in 1957. Humphrey Morrison Burkill, son of I.H. Burkill, had been born in the Director's House in the Gardens and became, until 1969, Gardens' Director himself. His was the first serious investigation of Malayan seaweeds. It was Burkill who saw the Gardens through the crucial transition from British leadership to 'Malayanization'.

Facing the challenges of an independent Republic in the mid-sixties, the new government looked to the Gardens for aesthetic as well as scientific support. Mustering over a century's botanical and horticultural know-how, the Gardens led in the campaign to create an environmental impact suitable to Asia's emerging business and financial centre – a 'Garden City'. Beautification of Singapore became the order of the day.

From an essentially research-oriented institution with responsibilities for the entire region, the Gardens' mission was revised to provide a botanical and horticultural service for Singapore. Ambitious tree-planting schemes were instituted. The plant sales nursery was expanded to step up supply of material for both public and private consumption. Tens of thousands of plants and advice on planting and layout of gardens were freely given to various government departments, schools, statutory boards, charitable institutions, and community centres.

Prime Minister Lee Kuan Yew celebrating the tenth annual Tree Planting Day, November 1980 in the Gardens. The tree being honoured is a young African Mahogany (*Khaya senegalensis*) located on Lawn A near the Main Gate Road and Marsh Garden.

All of these efforts to beautify Singapore culminated in the first 'Tree Planting Day' in November 1971. Again the Gardens played a major role in supplying the plant material and advice on the most advantageous locations for planting. This special, symbolic event continues to be celebrated annually in Singapore.

With the 'greening' of Singapore well under way, the Gardens turned to a programme of self-renewal in the late sixties and seventies. To enhance its attraction as a public park, a number of special features were added: the Miniature Waterfall, the Orchid Enclosure and Demonstration Centre, the Sundial Garden, the Japanese Garden, an Aviary, Ornamental Plant Houses devoted to cacti, succulents and tropical plants, and the second lake at Cluny Road.

The grounds were finally closed to automobile traffic. The old vine-covered gazebo at the Maranta Avenue entrance to the Jungle was brought over from the Old Admiralty House at Grange Road. New buildings were erected and old ones renovated to accommodate the still expanding Herbarium and Library collections and the new laboratory facilities for research.

Following Dr Chew Wee Lek's short term as Director, A.G. Alphonso, the Senior Curator under Burkill, took up the post of chief administrator. A Kew-trained horticulturist and most avid plant collector with special interest in propagating new, exotic hybrids, Alphonso carried on the Holttum tradition through his tenure (1970–76), furthering the Gardens' reputation as a world famous garden for the collection of orchid species, hybrids and advice on hybridization.

Princess Michiko admiring the *Dendrobium* Michiko named after her in 1970.

To assist local orchid growers and breeders and help cultivate Singapore's increasing enthusiasm for orchid hybrids, a Tissue Culture Laboratory was established in the early seventies. Using the meristem method of clonal propagation, great masses of plantlets could be produced in the Laboratory's controlled conditions that matched the quality and characteristics of the parent plants. By applying advanced biological techniques to the commercial propagation of orchids, Singapore's orchid growers could further expand an already successful local and export trade.

Apart from these technical advances, there was tremendous growth in planting and public horticultural work, including conferences, exhibitions and horticultural shows. Demands on the Gardens for educational and technical assistance increased. And in 1972 the new School of Ornamental Horticulture offered the first Diploma course in theoretical and practical training – taking the Gardens' educational mission a giant step further.

In 1973, the Botanic Gardens merged with the Parks and Trees Branch of the Public Works Division to form the Parks and Recreation Division, now a department under the Ministry of National Development.

Planting on into the Eighties

Notwithstanding its virtues as a splendid place for family outings or a retreat from the noisy world, the chief purpose of the Gardens is threefold – botanical, horticultural and educational, each contributing to and supported by the others. According to Mrs Ng Siew Yin, Assistant Commissioner of Parks and Recreation and Botanic Gardens Branch chief administrator since 1976, taxonomic studies and pure research have given way to the more practical objectives of applied botany and horticulture to meet the Republic's goals of a better environment. Today, the Gardens measures its successes in horticultural research, improving plant material, and providing a more aesthetic environment for Singapore.

The ongoing botanical activities of collection, identification

The extension of our Botanic

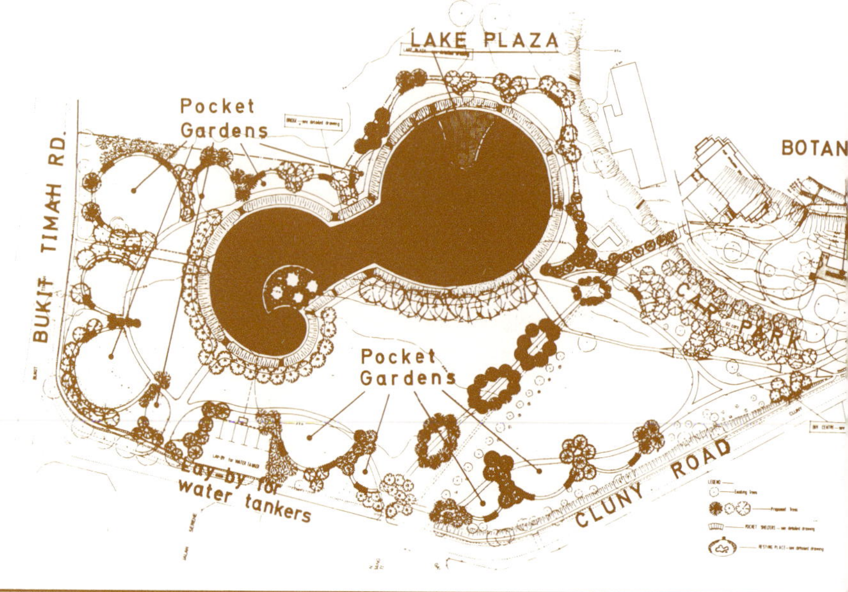

and international exchange of plant specimens remain the province of the Gardens' Herbarium. Together with the Library's holding of 20,000 volumes, these facilities continue to serve botanists as an important reference and lending centre for research on the region's flora. And the Gardens' journal, now under the title *Gardens' Bulletin, Singapore*, continues to broadcast original research and reviews of progress in the fields of botany, horticulture and allied subjects after nine decades' contribution to tropical plant knowledge.

The Gardens' large collection of living plants numbers over 2000 perennial specimens, not including hybrids, each one scientifically labelled for purposes of identification and study. These form a good representation of plant groups distributed throughout the world's tropical and sub-tropical regions, with particular concentration in palms and orchids.

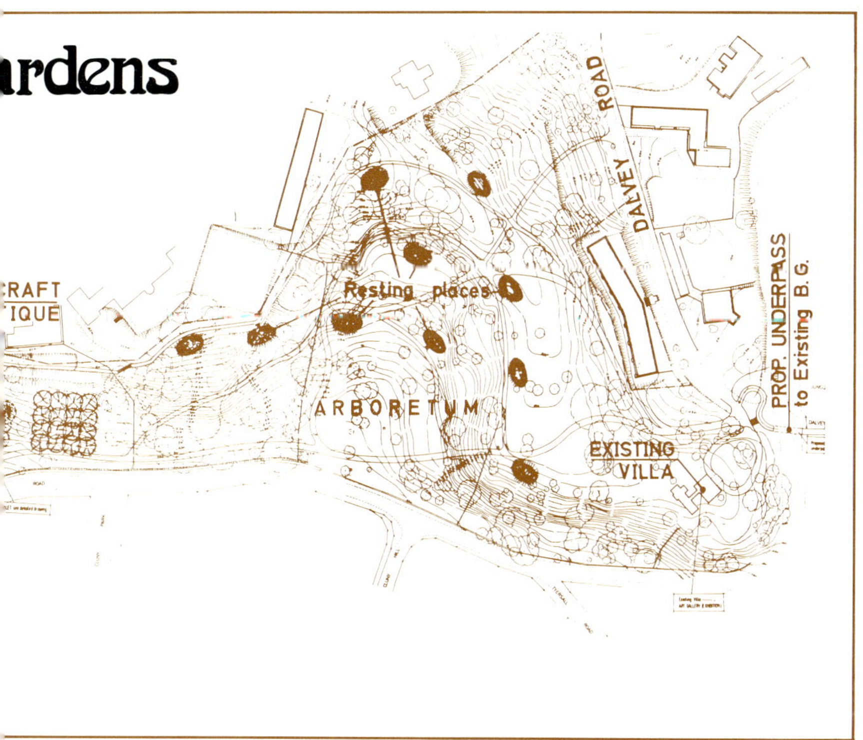

In terms of horticultural work, the Gardens introduces annually many new and exotic species of aesthetic and botanical interest and thousands of plants through exchange of seeds and cuttings with overseas institutions and individuals, and through plant collecting expeditions to places as far away as Central and South America. These add more colour and variety of flowering and ornamental species to the Garden City's parks, open spaces and roadsides.

At least a representative sample of each new plant material is tested under the ideal nurturing conditions provided in the Gardens' grounds. But long ago the Gardens outgrew its 34-hectare bounds and ceased functioning as a trial ground. In an effort to overcome these spacial limits to its growth, a proposed extension of 15 hectares will open sometime during the 1980s. Located to the north of the current grounds and incorporating a part of the old Economic Gardens, the extension will feature an arboretum including local tropical fruit trees and an exhibition hall which will serve as a learning centre.

Local growers and home gardeners look to the Gardens for the most current information and assistance in dealing with plant damage. A type of extension service is provided to anyone who wishes to come to the Gardens for identification of plant specimens or consultation on plant problems. Supported by laboratory and research facilities, the Research and Advisory Branch of the Parks and Recreation Department, working closely with the Gardens Branch, investigates the problems of insect damage, disease, and poor soil, and recommends remedial treatment or control measures.

The improvement and breeding of orchid hybrids has become a special study. Experimental work continues in search of the most ideal characteristics of size and shape of bloom, arrangement on the stalk, disease resistance, colour and proliferation of bloom, and so forth. And recent research in the Tissue Culture Laboratory has resulted in new and improved growing media that will effectively hasten the growth rate of orchid hybrids and many plant species.

A programme of self-fertilization of orchids is aimed at conserving our native species. And efforts are being made to conserve as much of the Gardens' native jungle as possible, in spite of the interferences and difficulties in maintaining ecological balance in so small a tract. Although certain species that die out cannot be replaced, wherever possible indigenous species are replanted.

Finally, the full mission of the Gardens – botanical, horticultural and educational – is incorporated in its School of Ornamental Horticulture. Now in its second decade, the School plays a most important role in the training of horticultural assistants and garden designers. Under the tutelage of the Gardens' curatorial staff, graduates of the School bring to the cultivation and care of the Island's greenery the latest research and practice of horticultural science.

Today, as on any day in the Botanic Gardens, schoolchildren huddle beneath the graceful branches of a tree, carefully examining the leaf and flower samples they have gathered. Meanwhile, in the Herbarium, a visiting scholar turns over the sheets of dried specimens preserved for over 175 years.

In other parts of the Gardens, maintenance work is being carried out by the 70-member gardening crew, some of whom represent their family's third generation in the Gardens. In one of the laboratories, trained technicians are handling sophisticated equipment used for growing countless orchid plantlets – derived from a species collected well over a century ago.

Flower-snipping culprits are still being reprimanded by the Park Rangers; curators are still advising visitors on age-old plant pests; strollers take their exercise round the Bandstand Hill; and the Gardens grows peaceably on.

A Stroll Through the Botanic Gardens

TODAY'S BOTANIC GARDENS encompasses an area of over 34 hectares (84 acres), originally virgin forest transformed into a park-like landscape of indigenous and new plant life. Over 2000 perennial specimens and countless hybrids largely of exotic origin flourish in the Gardens.

Wide sweeps of lawn break into terraces, marshes, rockeries, lakes and other scenic diversions. The roads and paths we shall follow are much the same as when they were laid out in the 1860s by the nutmeg planter Lawrence Niven, who must have had a gift for enduring landscape artistry.

The original tract (the bottle-shaped land exclusive of that portion west of Dalvey Gate Road and a narrow strip along Tyersall Road at the Lake) belonged to Hoo Ah Kay, better known as Whampoa, one of early Singapore's most influential and respected citizens. Himself a fancier of gardens, Whampoa traded his jungle plot at Tanglin for some port-side property – a more promising investment at mid-century.

Since that fateful transaction which brought a government grant of 23 hectares to the new Agri-Horticultural Society in 1859, adjoining tracts have been gained and lost and gained again; but the work of the Botanic Gardens has carried on.

What some 20,000 weekly visitors enjoy mainly as a recreational park is at its roots a *working* botanical garden where trained professionals collect, cultivate and distribute indigenous and exotic plants. It is a 'living museum' of treasures from the plant kingdom, exhibited and carefully identified with their scientific and common names and country of origin – a storehouse of plant information for researchers, educators, students and gardeners of every green persuasion. Through ongoing international exchange, new plants have been introduced to test their mettle in this one-season tropical soil; and some plants native to the region have found new homes in other world famous botanic gardens.

With sights set on the future, this oldest of Singapore's parks maintains its role as a training ground for Singapore's young horticulturists and as a laboratory where scientists from near and far come to observe the habits of plants, some fast disappearing from the green faces of the globe.

A botanist's laboratory, a horticulturist's dream – get ready for a visual extravaganza, an experience to re-kindle *all* the senses.

Main Gate Road Entrance

As we enter at the Main Gate Road, several majestic palms call us to attention. Immediately to our right, the Wild Date Palm (*Phoenix sylvestris*) grows stout and erect up to 18 metres with a roughly scalloped trunk. The luxurious spreading crown of arching, feathery leaves, 3 to 4 metres long, suggests Egypt's mythological bird. This 'phoenix of the forest' is widespread throughout India where it is used as a source of palm sugar.

Among the oldest inhabitants of the Gardens, the palm collection is one of the world's finest. The Palm Valley holds the most representative display, which we shall see further on Lawn W.

Best to start our walk in the early morning or late afternoon, lest we begin to droop like the Rain Tree (*Samanea saman*) behind the Wild Date Palm. This native of tropical America enjoys immense popularity in Singapore as a quick-growing shade tree for roads, open lawns and parks. It flowers in white to pink-tipped, fine brushy clusters and produces leathery black pods. The leaflets of the Rain Tree's widespread crown characteristically fold together at night. During the day, its droopy appearance is said to harbinger rain.

Rain Tree (*Samanea saman*)

Past the Gate and on the left, the low-growing tree *Brownea ariza* from Colombia exhibits velvet pods, flaming pink tassel-head inflorescences, and long, tapering, shiny leaves marked by a pale pink to brown buff colour in the new growth. By parting the overhanging leaves, you may duck inside this cool domed shelter and enjoy the privacy of a green hideaway.

The Browneas rest in the shade of the Sago Palm (*Metroxylon sagus*) whose trunks extend along the ground and then rise to clusters of 8 to 10 fronds branching from a central stem. Just before flowering, Sago Palms grown for commercial purposes are cut down and the trunks' inner pith rasped, freeing a starchy substance which is used as a flour in Malay desserts such as Gula Melaka. In Indonesia, beetles are attracted to the cut pith where they lay their eggs, and then the larvae are harvested as a source of protein.

Next on our route, the distinctive Traveller's Palm (*Ravenala madagascariensis*) opens enormous fans to the sky. Although often mistaken for a palm, this large plant from Madagascar with palm-like trunks is a banana ally and not a true palm at all. Thirsty natives of Madagascar drink the rain water trapped in the flower bracts and chambers formed by its overlapping sheaths. When the lower leaf sheaths of the plant are cut, water runs out.

Bright beds of various Canna hybrids in yellow, red and orange border the Main Gate Road. In the mid-nineteenth century, *Canna* species were known to grow as tall as 3.5 metres with small flowers and a bronze foliage. Today's Cannas are very much hybridized, certainly shorter, and display large, showy blossoms.

Let us cross the Main Gate Road and turn our attention to Lawn B. Keeping a constant glow of colour in the Gardens, the hardy scrambling shrub *Bougainvillea* is one of Singapore's most popular garden plants from tropical America. Named after the French explorer and scientist, Louis Antoine de Bougainville (1729–1811), its inconspicuous flowers are surrounded by conspicuously brilliant coloured bracts from white to deep purple, some 20 shades in all. The sun-loving Bougainvillea can be trained to form these individual shrubs or to climb supports, as you may have noticed along the Cluny Road fence.

Beyond the Bougainvillea grows a species of pine that numbers among the Gardens' wonders. The Cook Pine (*Araucaria cookii*) seems to lean at a precarious angle, like a green Tower of Pisa. In its natural home of New Caledonia, however, it grows straight as a pole and may attain 60 metres. Here it may be adjusting its pattern of growth to the prevailing winds, or to the work of white ants, or other local conditions – all of which remain matters of speculation.

Also on Lawn B, we can compare several species of *Casuarina*, named for their switchy twigs which resemble the Cassowary 'Kasuari' bird. *Casuarinas* are found growing in Australia for the most part, but also in Malaysia, Borneo and Indonesia. One

Cook Pine (*Araucaria cookii*)

typical example, the Common Ru (*Casuarina equisetifolia*) has rather uncommon-looking leaves resembling scales which encircle the drooping needle-like twigs and can be seen better with a magnifying glass. Grey-green to brown-green, this tall, graceful tree would appear to be most at home battered about on wind-swept ridges – where several species including the Bornean Ru (*Casuarina nobilis*) do make their homes.

Continuing along the Main Gate Road, on Lawn B you will notice a pair of Stag's Horn Fern (*Platycerium coronarium*) making a home in the Snake Tree. This epiphytic fern absorbs a tremendous amount of moisture through a fibrous root system and feeds on the humus of dead leaves held in a sort of basket formed by its erect fronds. Its pendulous fronds resemble the branching antlers of a stag. Several species of the Stag's Horn are found as far away as tropical America and as near to us as the

A Stag's Horn Fern (*Platycerium coronarium*) makes a home in the Snake Tree (*Stereospermum fimbriatum*) on Lawn B.

Bougainvillea shrubs on Lawn B and, at right, one of many varieties of *Bougainvillea*.

A bright *Canna* hybrid on Lawn A near the Main Gate.

Common Ru (*Casuarina equisetifolia*)

tall trees on Bukit Timah Hill. These ferns reproduce by spores which are carried by the wind to their high-perched destinations.

The hosting Snake Tree (*Stereospermum fimbriatum*) can be found from Burma to Malaysia. A tall, straight tree with a narrow crown, it is most easily distinguished by the loosely coiled pods that hang 36-60 cm long. After flowering, the trumpet-shaped pale lilac corollas with a fringed edging spin down from the tall crown and carpet the ground like thick snow-flakes, especially noticeable during a long period of drought.

Like many economic plants, early uses of the Snake Tree were multiple. In India the Snake Tree was an important source of timber, and in Malaysia juice was squeezed from the leaves into an aching ear or spread on itching skin. Malay women used to prepare a decoction from the roots to be taken after childbirth.

Further uphill, still on Lawn B, you may step inside a circular fortress of Yellow Bamboo (*Schizostachyum brachycladum*). Through the bars and sunlit leaves, we capture a different vision of the Gardens and perhaps can understand why Chinese poets and brush painters have found their inspiration in these tropical grasses. This species, the 'golden-stemmed' bamboo, is ornamental and comes from the Moluccas. Species from China are used in a vast array of constructions from bridges to blow-pipes, and ancient Chinese scholars used these hard-walled stems for their writing tablets. Please resist the urge to follow suit, as did one poor fellow here who was prompted to announce his heart's despair over being jilted. No matter how meaningful the message, scratching on the culms permanently disfigures the bamboo and spoils its beauty. Look for the most extensive collection of bamboo on the slope above the southeastern end of the Lake at Cluny Road (Lawn W).

Looking back across the Main Gate Road and downhill to Lawn A, we see the first of the Gardens' many fig trees, the Malayan Banyan (*Ficus retusa*). This naturally sculptured wonder stands on a leggy supporting structure of scattered prop roots. By producing hanging roots which thicken into pillars once they have reached the ground, the Malayan Banyan can extend over a wide area and support a canopy of long branches. Found from India to Australia, and down Western Malaysia to Singapore,

Malayan Banyan (*Ficus retusa*)

this fig prefers the wet ground of lowland swampy forests. The adventitious roots and leaves have been used in Asian folk medicines to treat toothaches, headaches, colic and bruises.

Behind the Banyan near Holland Road is an example of the famous Areca or Betel Palm (*Areca catechu*) whose 'nuts' have played accompaniment to so much social ritual in tropical Asia. The slender, rather tall Betel Palm displays a crest of only a few pinnate leaves and bright orange-red fruit. Probably originating in the Malay Peninsula, the Palm has been widely cultivated for its seeds which are chewed, either fresh or (more usually) cured with lime, betel pepper leaves and various seasonings. The mild stimulant or narcotic effects are said to relieve certain stomach disorders. Younger specimens of the *Areca* may be found on Lawn X near the Palm Valley.

The Marsh Garden

The water-loving plants that flourish in this naturally low-lying area on Lawn A take advantage of both the run-off and ground waters that seek this marshy bottom. Most arresting are the Siamese Screw-pines (*Pandanus kaida*) with their multiple prop roots forming a sort of skirted footing. Long cultivated in the Botanic Gardens, the woody *Pandanus* has been most valued for the fibre given by its tough, spiny leaves, growing to 4.5 metres and used in making sails, cloth, paper, brushes and ornamental streamers. In addition to medicinal uses, the younger flower spikes of certain *Pandanus* species when boiled in milk are said to brew a magic love potion!

Siamese Screw-pine (*Pandanus kaida*)

Another paper-making plant, Egypt's famed Papyrus (*Cyperus papyrus*) tosses its fountain-spray heads in this swampy habitat – along with a cousin of the same family, the Umbrella Plant (*Cyperus flabelliformis*).

The meandering paths around the ponds are designed to give you a dragonfly's eyeful of marsh plants: Sedges, Cattails, the arrow-headed Aroids, Red Ginger, Lilies and an occasional dragonfly.

At the far end of the Marsh Garden, the Indian Putat (*Barringtonia acutangula*) flowers in 30 cm long pendulous racemes and drops a scarlet powder of blooms on the Marsh Garden path. Near by is the Putat Laut (*Barringtonia asiatica*), a seashore tree common in the Peninsula and noted for its large leaves, flowers and fruit.

Broad-leaf Mahoganies (*Swietenia macrophylla*) from Honduras, a relative of the famous wood and a fine shade tree, grow along the Holland Road fence. Next to these is the Pig's Mango (*Terminalia phellocarpa*), a Malayan tree bearing mango-like fruit.

Also in the area between the Marsh Garden and Holland

Road are several evergreen Pong Pong or Buta Buta trees (*Cerbera odollam*). The bushy, rounded crown of large glossy leaves, its scented white flowers and distinctive fruit make this native tree one of the most beautiful and popular of Singapore's park and roadside trees. Although inviting, the flattened globes of shiny fruit, turning apple green to reddish black, are inedible, and the seeds and sap are poisonous.

Uphill near the Main Gate Road grows another common substitute for Mahogany. Richly coloured and beautifully figured wood when mature, this young African Mahogany (*Khaya senegalensis*) was planted by the Prime Minister, Mr Lee Kuan Yew, in November 1980 to commemorate the tenth Tree Planting Day – an event that has become an established tradition in the 'greening' of Singapore. In its native habitat, the African Mahogany reaches a height of 28 metres.

An Indian Rubber Tree (*Ficus elastica*) marks the triangle where the Main Gate Road meets the Lake-side path. From the eastern Himalayas to Java, this fig was cultivated as a source of rubber until it lost in competition with the much more elastic-sustaining Para rubber tree (*Hevea brasiliensis*). We shall see several examples of this famous crop later on.

The Indian Rubber is the same 'rubber tree' we are accustomed to growing as house plants, never imagining that taken out of their well-tended pots they might grow to the magnificent dark green leafy shade tree exhibited here.

Now that we have reached the southern end of the Lake, let us quench our thirst at the water fountain and take the foot-bridge to the shade provided by another widespreading fig (*Ficus kurzii*), wearing a thick girdle of pillar roots and the long hanging threads of aerial roots. The *Ficus* genus is second only to the *Eugenia* in having the largest number of species of woody plants in our region. Many different kinds of fig trees, both introduced and native to the region, are so plentiful that they form significant parts of the jungle, roadside and village landscapes — but less so now in Singapore.

Tembusu (*Fagraea fragrans*)

Some common characteristics of fig species are a smooth, pale bark, milky latex, leaves simple or lobed, and flowers hidden within the fig itself. Many have roots which hang down from the branches individually or in tassels like long brown string. Groups of figs are distinguished by their method of growth. 'Strangling Figs', such as *Ficus kurzii*, *F. retusa*, *F. elastica* and other Gardens' examples, may begin life by growing in the forks of other trees, then develop hanging and clasping horizontal roots that eventually surround the host with a lattice-work of supports. 'Stem Figs' produce bunches of figs growing out of the trunk and main branches. The fig is a composite fruit with seeds inside a fleshy receptacle which has a small opening at its apex where insects enter to pollinate the flowers. Some species are edible.

Back on the Main Gate Road and looking toward the convergence of paths separating Lawns B and E, we spy two enormous Tembusu (*Fagraea fragrans*), very tall and shapely trees native to the region. The trees flower twice a year, producing masses of tiny fragrant flowers followed by shiny scarlet berries which attract flocks of birds and flying foxes. Characterized by horizontal or basal limbs, the timber has given the durable wood for chopping blocks and the head and foot-posts of Muslim graves. For the beautiful form and hardness of the Tembusu, the Malays compare it metaphorically to a 'hard heart'. The tree on Lawn E was one of the Gardens' original inhabitants.

On the slopes above the Lake still stand many economic trees planted soon after the foundation of the Gardens in 1859. Not far from the road, a Rambai (*Baccaurea motleyana*) bears 'golden berries' – small, thin-skinned and velvety fruits with a translucent white pulp. An uncommon native tree, the Rambai is one of many species preserved in the Botanic Gardens. On the bank another early introduction, the Indian Mango (*Mangifera indica*), dips its branches into the Lake and provides a shady gathering spot for the Lake's water-fowl.

The Main Lake

Stocked with aquatic plants and fish, the Lake measures nearly 1.5 hectares and a depth of 1 to 3 metres. Peking ducks, white swans and black, gifts from Australia, and mute swans from Amsterdam keep the waters in constant motion. Feeding the water-fowl and fish is every child's delight. A few breadcrumbs will attract a noisy scramble of beaks, feathers and flashes of golden Japanese carp. The Lake's perches draw other birds native to the region, such as the Common Kingfisher with its prominent beak and spectacular blue plumage.

Birds you will notice most frequently on your trek through the Gardens include the bright yellow, flute-whistling Orioles, the black and white Pied Trillers, Brown-throated Sunbirds, *and* the ubiquitous Mynas. A variety of features attract these and other less common birds to the Gardens.

The Philippine Glossy Starling and many other species, for example, love the figs. A nectar-sucking bird with curved beak, the Brown-throated Sunbird prefers the red and brightly coloured flowers of the Hibiscus, the New Guinea Creeper and certain orchids. The Common Iora, a bright green and yellow bird, favours the *Casuarinas*.

Doves scratch the ground for seed, and the Mynas feed on ants. From its perches on the lower branches of the Tembusu or the Teak, the White-collared Kingfisher scans the lawns below for large insects, lizards and grasshoppers, while the Common Kingfisher goes diving for fish in the Lake. The White-breasted Waterhen, who walks on a pair of long legs with its short tail erect, also enjoys the Gardens' lakes, ponds and swampy places.

Now and again you will hear the loud, distinctive '*tiong*' whistle of the Hill Myna or 'Burong Tiong', one of Singapore's most valued cage-birds. The Tiong nests quite high in tall trees, preferably dead ones. The colourful little Tailorbird builds a rather curious nest of a single large living leaf curled round and laced together with spider's web and tree-cotton from the Kapok – the source of many birds' nesting materials.

Beyond a bird's requirements for food, water and shelter, a suitable habitat must offer proper breeding places. You may have noticed a number of nest boxes (birdhouses) of various shapes, sizes and passageways placed about the Gardens' trees. Behind this new experiment is the hope that more colourful, song and other preferred bird species will make homes in the Gardens.

The towering Nibong Palm (*Oncosperma tigillarium*) dominates the Lake's central islet. Native to the mangrove forests, this very hard, durable and elastic palm is used by local fishermen for fishing stakes. Pirates of the Archipelago shaped their lances from its trunk, and its spiny studs made excellent javelin-heads and darts for blow-pipes.

The Nibong Palm shares the tiny island with Siamese Screw-

Feeding time at the Main Lake.

Buds of the Sacred Lotus (*Nelumbo nucifera*) and a full bloom at the Lotus Pond.

pines and the decorative flowering shrub called Simpoh (*Dillenia suffruticosa*) – a quite vigorous and luxuriant evergreen with flowers 10 cm across of 5 yellow petals, and most conspicuous in the southern Malay Peninsula. The large leaves of the Simpoh shrub were used for wrapping local 'take-away' food until plastic wrappers replaced Nature's packaging.

Apart from being a major focal point in the Gardens, the Lake provides a most important service. Each morning water is pumped from its reservoir into the Parks and Recreation Department tankers and then transported all across Singapore to water thirsty plants, thereby conserving the City's drinking water.

In recent years there has been an annoying tendency for turtle fanciers to inflict their excess brood on the Lake. Thus an unmanageable number of turtles play havoc on both the waterfowl and the aquatic plants. Even so, this seems a minor nuisance compared to some of the larger reptile problems the Gardens has had to contend with. In 1892, during Ridley's tenure as Director, an escaped crocodile took up residence in the Lake. After a nasty attack on one of the gardeners, the Lake was completely drained and the creature summarily dispatched.

To the northeast of the Snack Bar on Lawn H are planted species of Australian *Araucaria* and a West Indian Locust Tree (*Hymenaea courbaril*), which dominates our view at the top of the hill. The leaves of the Locust Tree are paired in strongly asymmetric leaflets, thus taking the name of Hymen, the Greek god of marriage. This tall, quick-growing shade tree was introduced to Singapore from tropical America in 1875. Its hard resin gives an excellent copal varnish, but the flowers and bruised pods exude an unpleasant smell. You can see how the lower branches of this particular tree have developed as strongly as the main stem to present a low, widespreading crown on a short, massive trunk – not necessarily true of the species.

After we quench our thirst with a fresh lime drink and have a snack at the Snack Bar, let us carry along the Weeping Willow-lined bank between the Lake and the Lotus Pond. The pink-blushing Sacred Lotus (*Nelumbo nucifera*) over-shadows the waterlilies and other aquatic plants, and its blue-green leaves create a floating carpet across the pond. Much grown in the Orient for its edible seeds and rhizomes, the Lotus forms a staple in the local Chinese diet and is consumed for its cooling effect. The entire plant is also used medicinally.

On a more poetic note, the flower symbolizes purity and perfection, a thing of beauty whose roots are bound in mud. Sacred to Buddhists and Taoists, 'Lady Virtue', as the Lotus is known in Chinese classics, keeps her beauty hidden until late afternoon when she begins opening her petals to full brilliance for the eyes of night. By mid-morning, her shy petals close again.

Once across the Lake, we may turn right toward the Miniature Waterfall Garden or turn to our left and investigate the western bank and a variety of economic and medicinal plants on Lawn F – a paddock for deer prior to its planting in 1890.

Trees similar to the Jambu Laut (*Eugenia grandis*) that hugs the Lake's bank here would have been among the first to greet Raffles as he came ashore. This *Eugenia* has a dense obconic crown of shiny dark green leaves and grows large, fluffy white flowers three or more times a year. The Jambu Laut or Sea Apple is one of almost 200 species of *Eugenia*, the foremost genus of flowering plants in Malaya. These small to medium-sized trees may reach 20 metres and occupy a large portion of the tree growth below the forest canopy. Once quite abundant in the Straits Settlements, *Eugenias* were planted as fire-breaks along Dalvey Road and other main arteries, because the thick bark was known to withstand lalang fires.

Another 'Strangling Fig', the famous Indian Banyan (*Ficus benghalensis*) overhangs the Lake. This one produces tawny-rose figs in pairs without stalks, and the crown has been known to spread over 600 metres in individual specimens in India, where it is considered a sacred tree.

The Sea Teak (*Podocarpus polystachyus*), a coastal tree with horizontal limbs set with clusters of narrow leaves, is our most common wild Podocarp and a good timber tree. This species grows on rocky beaches and prefers life at sea-level.

Those massive lengths of rope you see growing into the Angsana on Lawn F belong to the climbing palm (*Calamus scipionum*). The long, hooked whips of stem enable the plant to climb as much as 4.5 metres. If ever you must extricate yourself from the lethal-looking thorns, remember that they grow backwards on the sheaths, so it is best to step back rather than pull forward. This Malacca Cane Plant, or forest rattan (*rotan*), refers to many *Calamus* species that with other climbing palm genera are used in the making of so much local cane furniture.

The Angsana (*Pterocarpus indicus*) supporting the cane is another tree with heavily-scented yellow flowers that burst all at once into blossom and then rain down next morning. The wood has a pleasant smell and is used in decorative carving and cabinet making. A tree known for its vast shady crown and easy growth, the Angsana has been propagated for some time in Singapore as an 'instant tree'.

Finally we reach the grassy triangle where the Purple Millettia (*Millettia atropurpurea*) drops pods which look like polished chunks of fine-grained wood. Originating in Burma, Thailand and Malaysia, this large, handsome tree produces deep reddish purple flowers in terminal panicles. Its roots grow next to Burma's Chaulmoogra Tree (*Hydnocarpus kurzii*). The velvet-coated seeds of the *Hydnocarpus* produce an oil used in the treatment of leprosy.

Back at the Lake's divide and passing the Lotus Pond on our right, we might imagine Tarzan swinging from the liane that seeks its support across the path in the Sengkawang (*Shorea sumatrana*). Lianes, stout woody climbers, are a familiar attraction in the Island's primary and secondary forests – sometimes growing into fantastic shapes.

The Waterfall Garden

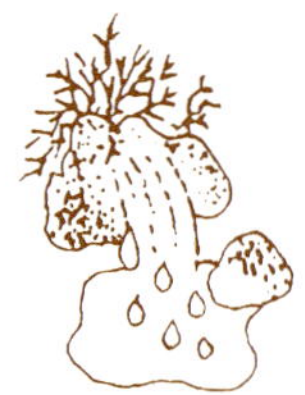

We should feel a welcome coolness as we enter the Waterfall Garden, constructed around the stream which feeds the Lake. Here the temperature drops by several degrees and the sounds change, too – from the low, almost imperceptible croak of pond frogs to the high-pitched whirr-whistle of the cicadas. Through a labyrinth of short paths and rocky crevices harbouring arrow-headed Aroids, Begonias, ferns and gingers, your ear will lead you to the gentle music of the Miniature Waterfall. The cascading waters feed the Lake and help recreate the lush greenery common to Singapore's jungle streams.

Notable among the species growing here are the local stemless 'Elephant Fern' (*Angiopteris evecta*) with large fronds and long leaflets, the Fishtail Palm (*Caryota mitis*) and a grand example of Sri Lanka's Fern-leaf Tree (*Filicium decipiens*). The jaunty red Cardinal's Guard (*Pachystachys coccinea*) from the West Indies, several species of *Heliconia*, also from tropical America, Red Gingers (*Alpinia purpurata*) from Polynesia and the unusual black, long-whiskered Bat Lily (*Tacca integrifolia*) from Southeast Asia provide flashes of colour amongst the prevailing green. These plants have been chosen for their wealth of ornamental features and ability to thrive in a very moist environment. They play a major role in keeping the Waterfall Garden as dense, shady, humid and 'wild' as possible.

Any one of several paths through this thick foliage will take us back to the main road and the root-strewn slopes of Lawn H. With branches that sweep the ground, the rare species *Alangium ridleyi* spreads ribbon roots in lavish abundance. Named after its discoverer and Gardens' Director H.N. Ridley, this big tree is native to Singapore.

At the crest of the hill are two examples of a South American fruit and timber tree, the Monkey Pot (*Lecythis ollaria*). One of the early introductions to the Gardens, the Monkey Pot produces a large woody fruit opening by a lid that falls from the bottom. These are the sapucia or paradise nuts of commerce, also popular with monkeys and other animals. Just below these grows a native fruit tree, the Monkey Jack (*Artocarpus rigida*).

The Topiary

Forming a small triangle of lawn between Lawn H, Lawn G and Lawn S, the Topiary displays the special talents of the Gardens' landscape artists. Neatly clipped shrubs of *Carmona retusa* are trained and sculpted on wire supports to create the decorative shapes of the world's animal kingdom. An elephant, a crocodile, a tail-wagging dog and an eagle poised on the edge of flight are some of the creatures under the watchful eye of the Topiary's keeper. He is the one in the hat smoking a pipe and carrying a thick walking stick!

This menagerie serves as a reminder of the Gardens zoo which had a short but dramatic career from 1875 to 1905. Introduced as an educational attraction, the zoo grew to include 144 exhibits, many of them gifts – such as a leopard from the King of Siam, and a tiger from the Sultan of Trengganu. In 1875 the Acclimatisation Society in Melbourne sent an emu, 4 kangaroos, and a bushy-tailed wallaby. Expenditures far exceeded the government grant to maintain the animals, and gradually by death, misfortune, sale or gift, the animal population faded to a few birds and monkeys. In spite of the record number of globe-trotters the animals attracted in those days, the Gardens staff must have wondered if they were running a gardens or a zoo!

Past the Topiary on the main road, your eyes will fasten on a lane of five spectacular, tall Cannon-ball Trees (*Couroupita guianensis*) whose trunks are set with long twigs bearing fleshy flowers and 'cannon-ball' fruit. The globose, woody fruit up to 20 cm in diameter contains many seeds in a soft, ill-smelling pulp. The spicy fragrance and beauty of the large flowers of 6 unequal petals, salmon red on the inside and a waxy cream-yellow on the outside, are year-round pleasures found in the Gardens. Indigenous to the Guianas, a region in northeastern South America, the remarkable tree came to the Gardens in the form of seeds from a sister Botanic Garden, Sri Lanka's Peradeniya.

Past the Cannon-ball Trees, we come to the juncture where six paths meet, 'Six Ways'. Straight ahead, the Souvenir Kiosk has a good supply of film, hats, other odds and ends and a variety of drinks. But let us come back to it later upon return from our trek through the Palm Valley. Two floral islands display the fireworks of the red-stemmed cluster palm (*Cyrtostachys lakka*) encircled by flowering shrubs and bright annuals. Pinang Rajah or Sealing Wax Palm is one of those palms which branch at or under ground level. This native of our swamp forests also goes by the vernacular name, 'Lipstick Palm'. Look for its waxy red leaf sheaths and petioles throughout the Gardens and mainly at the Lower Ring Road where the palm forms an avenue.

The Cannon-ball Tree (*Couroupita guianensis*) on Lawn P and (left) a closer view of the Cannon-ball flower, a year-round pleasure in the Gardens.

1 Sowing seeds on agar
in a flask

2 Transfer of seedlings
to new flasks

3 Seedlings are removed
from flasks

4 Washing agar from
seedlings

5 Planting seedlings in
a community pot

6 General view of a
young orchid nursery

In the Orchid Enclosure. *Vanda* Miss Joaquim, Singapore's national flower.

The Topiary seen from Lawn H.

The woody fruit of the Monkey Pot (*Lecythis ollaria*) on Lawn H.

The Orchid Enclosure

All of Lawns P and R are devoted to the most famous family of plants in Singapore's Botanic Gardens – Orchidaceae. Well-known for its pioneering work in species collection, cultivation and hybridization, the Gardens holds a colour spectacle of captivating blooms, all carefully grown and nourished to peak performance.

At the entrance to the Enclosure, Singapore's national flower *Vanda* Miss Joaquim seems a fitting introduction to the multi-colour orchid display. Imagine the pleasure and surprise Agnes Joaquim must have experienced upon discovering this delicate mauve beauty, a new creation growing in the full sun of her garden. The progeny of two local parent species, this very free-flowering natural hybrid appeared in 1893.

Since the origins of the Gardens at Tanglin, orchid cultivation has been vigorously pursued, along with an enthusiastic programme of species exchange. In 1928 R.E. Holttum, Director of the Gardens, recognizing both the popular and commercial desire for orchid species of aesthetic merit, launched a programme of extensive hybridization using local stud plants from the jungle. New Singapore-grown, free-flowering orchid blooms have been showing their faces in major commercial ports of the world ever since.

Several stages in the process of orchid breeding, from pod collection to flask culture to full-flowering plant can be observed in photographs at the Orchid Demonstration Centre in the Orchid Enclosure. Samples of live plant specimens show the maturing orchid through one to four years of patient care.

In the Gardens' Tissue Culture Laboratory, successful techniques for the propagation of desirable orchids have been developed under the meristem culture system. Tissue from selected parent plants are extracted, sterilized, sealed in a special nutrient medium supplemented with growth hormones, and then agitated in a shaker to insure cell multiplication. The resulting cloned progeny are exact replicas of the parent plant.

Along with *Vanda* Miss Joaquim, countless specimens of hybrids including those named after visiting dignitaries are on display. One of the fascinations of the Orchid Enclosure is in identifying the famous names attached to these remarkable blooms: *Dendrobium* Elizabeth, after Her Majesty Queen Elizabeth II; *Dendrobium* Tsutako Nakasone, after the wife of Japan's Prime Minister; *Aranda* Imelda Romualdez Marcos, after the Philippines' First Lady, and many other orchids named after international notables past and present who have found pleasure in the Gardens.

Just one last eye-catcher here – the Tiger Orchid or Giant Orchid (*Grammatophyllum speciosum*), an epiphyte of the Malay archipelago and the world's largest orchid plant. If you are fortunate enough to visit the Gardens in its flowering season, you will see as many as 60 long spikes of tiger-spotted flowers opening at the same time on this shy bloomer. Back in the nineteenth century, the one-ton parent plant was collected near Penang and then divided. One half reached the Columbian Exposition in Chicago where it created quite a sensation and the other half took up residence on a Rain Tree in the Singapore Botanic Gardens. The orchid managed to outlive the hosting Rain Tree and was divided into several parts which may be seen here and on Lawns E and K.

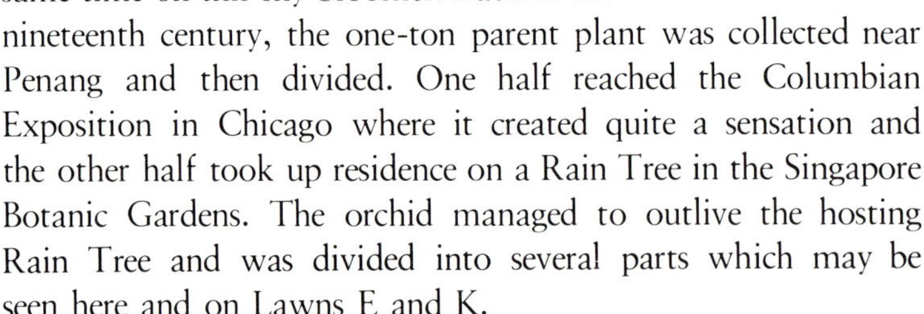

The Gardens' orchid plants and plantlets may be purchased at the nearby kiosk or at the Office annex.

Two 'true' Mahoganies (*Swietenia mahogani*) skirt the fence outside the entrance to the Orchid Enclosure. This West Indian Mahogany from Jamaica, a slow grower in this region, has been known from the earliest days of trans-Atlantic sailing as the foremost timber for shipbuilding and repairing, as well as a premier cabinet wood of the world. Near these, the Paper-bark Tree or Cajeput (*Melaleuca leucadendron*) from northern Australia, New Guinea and the Moluccas peels a flaky bark that with the aid of a dammar resin was useful to Malays of old as a torch. The leaves of this species also yield a greenish aromatic oil called 'cajeput'. Look for another specimen of this *Melaleuca* behind the Snack Bar.

School of Ornamental Horticulture

As we leave the Orchid Enclosure and turn to our left, the path uphill through the gates leads to a spacious yard and bungalow constructed in 1866 for the Superintendent of the Gardens. Today it houses the School of Ornamental Horticulture.

With the gradually developing concept of Singapore as a 'Garden City' came the demand for expertise in the field of tropical horticulture. To meet this demand, the School opened its doors in 1972 to offer a two-year diploma course. Since that time, it has expanded to include three basic courses: both full and part-time diploma courses in Ornamental Horticulture and Garden Design, and a part-time certificate course in Ornamental Horticulture. Also gardening enthusiasts can take advantage of a number of 'how-to' home gardening classes offered to the public periodically. For information on these courses, be sure to inquire at the School.

Ornamental Plant Houses

Across the road from the entrance to the Orchid Enclosure, a footpath winds uphill through the dry beds and cacti-lined ridges of a Sun Rockery. The path takes us to the Ornamental Plant Houses, designated display areas which portray important plant groups with very specialized features, requiring special conditions for growth.

At the hilltop and just behind the rare, fork-branching Gingerbread Palm (*Hyphaene indica*), the first small octagonal structure holds a collection of Bromeliads. This family of mostly epiphytic plants from tropical America includes the pineapple, Spanish moss, and many species grown as houseplants. Sun-loving plants, they retain moisture in the spiralling rosettes formed by their long, stiff leaves. One of the most curious Bromeliads, the Fingernail Plant (*Neoregelia spectabilis*), appears to be wearing scarlet polish on the leaf tips.

The FOLIAGE HOUSE exhibits various shade plants which occur naturally in tropical jungles and are best suited to Singapore's humid climate. Since they prefer high atmospheric humidity but subdued light, the protective lathed roofing has been constructed to reduce the intensity of light and achieve a partially shaded environment.

Philodendron and *Monstera* climbing in the air-well and beds of *Spathiphyllum*, with white-tongued spathes enclosing thick spikes of flowers, represent a few of the Aroids grown here. Home gardeners will identify the Asparagus 'fern', the silver-edged *Peperomia*, the hairy Carpet-plant (*Episcia*), the long, leather-leafed *Cordyline*, and a shy blooming *Neomarica* species of the Iris family. Species of the ginger, arrowroot, *Agave*, Aroid, pepper and *Gesneria* families are well represented here.

An arrow points our way past a lawn sharpened with the vibrant colours of the Beefsteak Lobster Claw (*Heliconia mariae*) to the CACTI HOUSE. Here the sunlight shines through a roof designed to simulate the dry, hot atmospheric conditions suitable for the Cactaceae and other families of succulent plants. These residents of arid tropical and subtropical zones have been introduced here and elsewhere in the Gardens' sun rockeries to give a good representation of important plant groups not otherwise observable in this region.

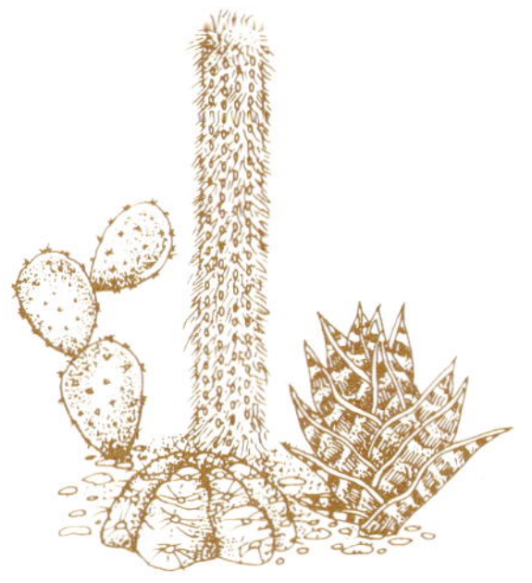

Not to be confused with the Cactaceae family from the arid zones of America, the Euphorbiaceae is a family which also has many species of succulents. Although *Euphorbia* has stems which are often spiny and cactus-like, this 'bull-with-milk' produces distinctive pairs of minute thorns and a milky sap that may blister the skin in susceptible individuals. The juice of some species is used as an arrow poison.

Some succulents have medicinal value as well. The compact rosette leaves of the *Aloe*, a species of succulents native to arid parts, chiefly Africa, contain a yellow juice well known as both a purgative and a soothing skin ointment. Leaves of the *Agave* and the *Yucca* make strong fibrous material. *Agave americana*, commonly known as the Maguey or Century Plant, is cultivated for the sap which in Mexico is distilled for mescal and tequila. Hooked spines edge the sword-shaped blue-green leaves of this *Agave* species. After ten years or more the plant sends a tall stalk of yellow-green flowers up to 12 metres in the air. Look for these and more succulents on Lawn E, Sun Rockery.

The path from the Cacti House leads us past a slope of Red Ginger, and on our left past a palm that is native to Southeast Asia – the large, saw-tooth leafed Gebang Palm (*Corypha elata*) just outside the TEMPERATE HOUSE. Museums contain paper documents made from the Indian *Corypha* which have been determined to be over 1000 years old.

The drawn blinds and sequestered look of the last Ornamental Plant House warn us not to disturb the delicate habitat created for these cool climate plants. We are permitted, however, to circle the protective enclosure of the Temperate House and peer through the moist glass onto blue African Violets (*Saintpaulia ionantha*), trails of Ivy (*Hedera helix*), and most curious of all, the Lady's Slipper Orchid. Slipper-lipped *Paphiopedilum* species, mottled or striped yellow to lavender, is the feature attraction here, along with other lowland and mountain-growing orchids.

Palm Valley

At the bottom of the hill, we are confronted with more evidence of the Gardens' topographical splendour. Here the land falls away into a valley swept with princely palms and rises beyond in a gentle slope finished with a woody skyline of tall jungle trees. Ranging in size from the squatty Mexican Fan Palm (*Washingtonia robusta*) to the skyscraper *Livistonas*, the Palm Valley collection ranks among the finest in the world.

Palms are chiefly tropical evergreen trees or shrubs having solitary or clustered trunks and pinnate (feather-shaped) or palmate (hand-shaped) leaves. From the majestic stance of this prize of the plant kingdom, it is easy to see why the palm has been the emblem of joy and triumph since ancient times.

Many of these handsome ornamental trees are also important

The Sun Rockery of cacti and other succulents on Lawn E.

The Palm Valley and a view of the Second Lake on Lawn W.

economic plants. To show the variety of possible uses, former Gardens' Botanist C.X. Furtado (1923–60) took the classic example of the Coconut Palm (*Cocos nucifera*). It is possible, he pointed out, not only to make a boat from its trunk, but also to provide the vessel with ropes, sails, cloth, flour, oil, sugar, wine, vinegar, spoons, brushes, brooms, drinking vessels, etc. – all derived from various parts of the tree.

The tangle of branches we meet as we step off the Temperate House path onto Palm Valley Road is – yes – a palm. The hooks of long-whipped *Calamus fasciculatus* (a relative of the Malacca Cane) enable this palm to climb 100 metres or more. Notice the rather lethal-looking thorny stems which would make collecting the cane a rather arduous task.

One of the most unusual palms, the Double Coconut (*Lodoicea maldivica*) produces the largest and heaviest seed in the plant kingdom. This half-metre long fruit resembles a pair of coconuts joined in Siamese twin fashion and weighs 13-18 kg. The fruit requires up to six years for full maturity, and the tree itself is especially slow-growing, rarely flowering before its thirtieth birthday.

The earliest mariners first encountered the giant nuts they called 'coco-de-mer' afloat in the sea. Thus fantastic legends grew about their source, one claiming that these plant goliaths came from a big tree growing in the navel of the Indian Ocean, unreachable because of fierce storms. Their mythical charm undoubtedly enhanced their supposed medicinal value, too. Credited with supplying a positive antidote for all forms of poison, these nuts brought huge sums during times when poison was the most fashionable means of dispensing with one's enemies. Even as late as the mid-eighteenth century, a double coconut fruit sold for around S$4000!

Double Coconut palms are found growing by the thousands only on the Seychelles Islands. Even though their seeds have been scattered widely by the oceans, they do not germinate on foreign shores. A few specimens can be found around the world's botanic gardens. Singapore's Botanic Gardens possesses two of these extremely rare plants, one located south near Dalvey Gate Road in the Palm Valley and one near the Office complex on Lawn K. By the way, their source name has been incorrectly attributed to the Maldives, and although they are called 'Double Coconut', the *Lodoicea* palm is not closely related to the *Cocos* genus.

Another prize among palms in the Valley, the Talipot Palm (*Corypha umbraculifera*) has the largest inflorescence of any flowering plant. After several decades of growth, the 'umbrella-bearing' Talipot will develop huge branches of flowers shaped like drooping ostrich plumes at the crown. Once it has achieved this feat of flowers — as many as 60 million on one tree — the Talipot will fruit and then die. Just as it prepares for flowering, natives of Sri Lanka and southern India, where it is widely cultivated, tap the Talipot for sugar. The juice is sweet and with fermentation may be turned into a toddy.

The Palm Valley has a good selection of the 24 species of *Livistona* – tall, fine-crowned Fan Palms familiar in many Malayan towns. Probably the most popular of all the fan palms, *Livistona chinensis*, originates in central China, where for centuries it has been used for making fans. The Chinese Fan Palm

can be recognized by its numerous fine leaflets, usually deeply forked and drooping at the tips, forming a sort of fringe effect around the leaves. The small blue-green fruit attract birds and small mammals, especially flying foxes.

One of the most common roadside trees in Singapore, the MacArthur Palm (*Ptychosperma macarthurii*) forms clusters 2 to 5 metres tall with slender, prominently ringed stems and broad pinnate leaves which carry serrated blunt-tipped leaflets. Native to Australia and New Guinea and named after Sir William MacArthur of New South Wales, son of the Australian botanist Captain John MacArthur, this species was brought to the Gardens in the late nineteenth century on its way to the fashionable conservatories of Victorian England. The Gardens planted a few; the birds fed on the bright orange fruit and dispersed the seeds; and the results can be seen in hedgerows throughout the Tanglin area near the Gardens. The MacArthur Palm and other species of *Ptychosperma* grow well as pot palms and their dense clusters can be made to form protective hedges.

Discussion of the more important palms here would not be complete without mentioning the famous African Oil Palm (*Elaeis guineensis*). This very successful economic palm was introduced in the region in the mid-nineteenth century, and by the 1970s covered some 300,000 hectares of Malaysia. The wall or fibrous pericarp of the fruit, which clusters 1500 strong on a tree, yields a clear, orange-coloured oil most useful in the manufacture of soaps, candles and lubricating greases. The oil of the kernel, however, is similar to the edible variety of coconut oil.

Scottish missionary and explorer, David Livingstone, is said to have distributed oil palm seeds among the African tribes he visited, with the hope of developing an industry that would keep workers at home. In fact, to the success of the African Oil Palm has been credited the eventual demise of Africa's slave trade.

Palm Valley Road

Following the Palm Valley Road downhill, let us focus on the left-hand bank where we find another economic plant from Africa. Making a web of roots on the hillside, the Kola-Nut (*Cola nitida*) is the tree that produces the flavouring in cola beverages. Since remote times, natives of West Africa's Ivory Coast have chewed the wild 'nut' for its tonic effect, similar to coffee and tea in other parts of the world. The kola-nut contains caffeine and a glucoside, and its bitter taste turns the flavour of food and drink sweet in the mouth. Plants introduced from Kew Gardens in Singapore in 1881 have grown well and fruited with regularity.

The left hillside is planted with several local species of Podocarps, valued for their timber and their ornamental beauty. The Malayan Yellow-Wood (*Podocarpus imbricatus*) may grow to 30 metres in the mountain forest but seldom to more than 12 metres here in the open. The crown may be conical or cylindrical and filled out with two types of leaves: on the lower branches, leaves shaped like the teeth of a comb; on the upper twigs, needle-like leaves set spirally. The Mountain Teak (*Podocarpus neriifolius*) resembles the Sea Teak we saw earlier on Lawn F, except that the leaves are coarser. The Mountain Teak also inhabits coastal regions.

Some 75 species of Podocarps are native to the temperate southern hemisphere, to the tropical mountains, and north to the East Indies and Japan. Their distinctive leaves are flat, spirally arranged, narrow and persistent.

Next to the Podocarps, *Cycas rumphii* might pass for a member of the palm family. Despite its palm-like crown of long, pinnate leaves, this is a modern representative of an ancient group of cone-bearing plants. This 'sea fern' grows wild along the region's seashores, and its large cones are dried and used in a poultice for sores.

The Second Lake

This lake offers an advantage over the first. Here we can walk out to the largest of three islands, a favourite site for band concerts. On a grass-covered lawn, some familiar friends pose in formal landscape arrangements: the Sealing Wax and Nibong Palms, Bird's Nest Fern, leafy clusters of bamboo, ornamental shrubs and flowers. Surrounding the islands, Waterlilies of blue (*Nymphaea capensis*), lemon yellow (*Nymphaea mexicana*) and every rainbow colour emerge out of the water between stepping-stone pads.

The arrow in the lake simply provides a point of reference today. In 1914, however, it marked the spot selected by the Carnegie Institute in Washington, D.C. to observe the earth's magnetism. The sign gives the coordinates of the marker's original position, or 1° 18.9′ N (Lat.) by 103° 48′ E (Long.).

Heading north again on Palm Valley Road, on our left past the access road we find an example of the Sacred Garlic Pear (*Crateva religiosa*) from India, where it is used to make a potent amulet. In Tahiti, the tree is often planted near temples. Among flowering trees, the Sacred Garlic Pear is especially desirable for the novelty it offers in ornamental planting. The flowers of five cream-coloured petals and many long violet stamens recall the peacock's feather-spread in miniature.

Be sure to keep your distance from the Rengas (*Semecarpus curtisii*) growing just behind the *Shorea macroptera* and extending its leafy branches over Palm Valley Road. Those familiar with the local lowland jungle carefully avoid this wild-growing species and its poisonous resin. Rain dripping from the Rengas may carry poison to the skin, causing mild itching or painful blisters and open sores that heal slowly. In habit and leaf, it is like the Mango tree, but a good guide to recognition of the Rengas is the black sap stains on the surface of the trunk and limbs – although other trees such as the Mangosteen also stain in a similar way.

Behind the Rengas stands a lofty triple-trunk structure, the native Meranti Paang (*Shorea bracteolata*) which occurs in the lowland forests and throughout the Malay Peninsula. Its small yellow flowers shower the ground in a wide circumference and broadcast a delicate fragrance. The *Shorea* directs the eye uphill toward an extension of Lawn Z, a well-established part of the Gardens that is seldom explored.

Near the second Marsh Garden stands a most unusual pair of tree-like shrubs introduced from New South Wales. The sun-loving Bottle Brush (*Callistemon lanceolatus*) does resemble that familiar kitchen tool. It flowers in drooping cylindrical spikes with masses of brilliant crimson brush-like stamens and dark yellow anthers.

The path skirting the lower end of the lake, past the marsh and its thick grove of Nibongs, is lined with bamboos and trees of largely ornamental value. One species of Common Bamboo especially worthy of note here, 'Buloh Gading' as the Malays call it, appears to have been touched up by an artist's hand. On each waxy yellow stem, fine-lined brush strokes of dark green accent the surface and vertical thrust of the bamboo.

Spaced judiciously between clumps of bamboo are especially

showy plants and a number of rather interesting foreign introductions. The Elephant Apple (*Dillenia indica*), for example, is unusual in its orange, flaking bark and massive 'apples' up to 18 cm wide. The flowers with five white petals are larger than those of any other Malayan tree and face downwards under the cover of large, glossy and distinctively ribbed leaves. The acid fruit of this 'Indian Simpoh' is edible when fresh and used in Indian curries and jellies called 'Chulta'.

The Elephant Apple's neighbour is one of the Gum Trees that can tolerate the wet climate of Singapore. Eucalypts include over 200 known species and are the most characteristic element of Australia's flora. This species, *Eucalyptus deglupta*, has the smooth, peeling bark generally associated with Gum Trees and thrives on reclaimed land here.

Over the red bridge and past the unusual golden glow of the *Melaleuca* shrub's foliage, we have several ornamental introductions from tropical America. A pair of Sea Grape (*Coccoloba uvifera*) flourish wide heartshaped leaves, red-veined and leathery in texture. This beachcomber from southern Florida to South America produces purple fruit resembling bunches of grapes which is used to make jelly. The *Gustavia superba* belongs to the same family as the dramatic Cannon-ball Tree, both conspicuous in their showy flowers and strong fragrance.

Para Rubber Monument

By now we have rounded the second lake and are headed back in the direction of the Palm Valley. Soon we should come to the area of the left bank where the Botanic Gardens' most famous economic product is planted. An important landmark in Singapore's history as well, the monument commemorates the introduction of the first Para rubber (*Hevea brasiliensis*) seedlings from Brazil to Singapore in 1877. The small monument, showing Ridley's herring-bone method of 'milking' the rubber trees, serves as a reminder of the Gardens' contribution to a vast industry that brought so much prosperity to the region.

Representative clones from Indonesia, Malaysia, the Philippines, Thailand, and Singapore are clustered here in diplomatic tribute to a common benefactor. And to the right of the monument stand seven young rubber trees. Older, well-established examples of the Para rubber may be seen on Lawn C, not far from the Office.

After paying our respects to 'Mother Rubber', let us scramble up the hillside past a collection of bamboo species. Among these grasses representing species cultivated throughout Asia, the most common village bamboo (*Bambusa vulgaris*) grows wild in the Malay Peninsula. Open clumps grow up to 20 metres in height and 13 cm in diameter and are often located on river banks. Common Bamboo represents only one of about 100 species of stout, tall, clump-forming perennial grasses with erect woody stems, ringed joints and sometimes spines.

In this area of the second lake, beside a generous display of Common Bamboo, we find the slender green *Schizostachyum jaculans* of Thailand and West Malaysia, the widely planted Yellow Bamboo (*Schizostachyum brachycladum*) of the Moluccas, and the densely tufted, grey-green *Thyrsostachys siamensis* of Thailand and Burma that peels a papery leaf sheath. From China are the ornamental Hedge Bamboo (*Bambusa glaucescens*), the Punting Pole Bamboo (*Bambusa tuldoides*) – important economically for its strong culms, and the clump bamboo (*Bambusa ventricosa*) known as 'Buddha's Belly'.

Apart from their value as ornamentals, the larger species produce stems used as timber and sources of paper pulp; one

The old vine-covered gazebo at the entrance to the Gardens' jungle.

Culms of Yellow Bamboo (*Schizostachyum brachycladum*) on Lawn B.

The Gardens' jungle

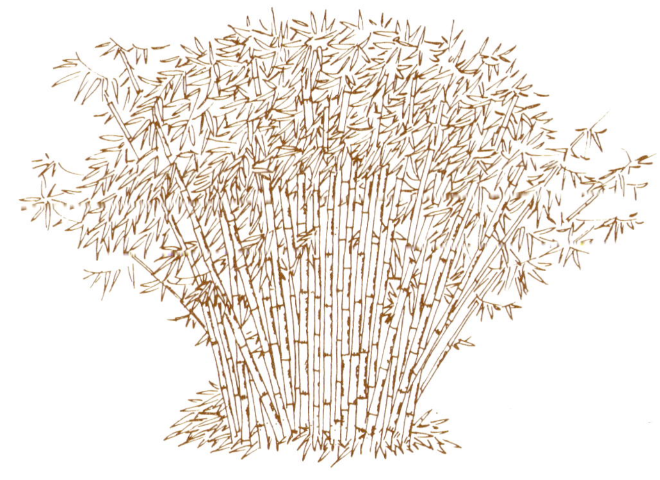

example is India's *Bambusa tulda* which is also outstanding in furniture and articles requiring split bamboo. The young stem sprouts, or 'bamboo shoots', of some varieties are edible. Bamboo is grown for erosion control, as hedges and ground cover, and in tubs and pots for the patio.

Now we follow the dense jungle line along Dalvey Gate Road back to the Souvenir Kiosk. Time out for some refreshment before we make our safari into the Gardens' jungle.

Wherever we go in the Gardens, we are likely to see members of the Gardens' maintenance crew at work – some 70 gardeners, tree pruners, carpenters, masons, sign writers, drivers, overseers – the people who diligently keep the grounds and plants in attractive and manageable order.

Take a look at the tools they are using. Some are as modern and noisy as the diesel-power age; others, as old and quiet as the gardening profession. It seems the best rakes and hand implements are made of bamboo poles, twigs, palm fronds and other parts the trees discard.

The Gardens' Jungle

At the jaunty old vine-covered gazebo that decorates the hillside off Maranta Avenue we enter the jungle. Next to the Bukit Timah Nature Reserve, this is one of the last vestiges of the Island's original evergreen forest – four hectares of virgin woodlands, preserved in the midst of the world's second busiest port city. For those of us who have no opportunity of penetrating the great Malayan forests, the Gardens' jungle offers a gentle introduction to a part of the earth's most complex habitat.

The broad canopy of trees, some rising to over 50 metres – countless species of plants, many rarely seen in our urban world – and the brooding stillness all remind us of an ancient yet delicate life that hangs in a balance fast tipping toward extinction of many species, as forests such as this one are cleared. Some botanists predict that all tropical forests will vanish by the end of this century – and with them new, regenerative sources of fuel, hope for curative medicines, and a whole 'library' of genetic information just barely explored from which humanity can learn.

What at first appears to be an enormous variety of different kinds of plants growing in haphazard confusion actually forms a balanced organization of plants in definite relation to one another. Governing the whole organization, the loftiest trees interlock branches and form a continuous canopy, casting shade on all the plants below. The Dipterocarps, of which *Shorea* forms the largest genus, rise to 30 metres or more, straight and unbranched below the spreading crown.

Layer upon layer, lesser trees such as the *Eugenia* complete the under-storeys. On the forest floor, the lowest layer of plant life prevails in the greatest shade – shrubs, small palms, gingers, ferns, herbaceous plants, and the seedlings of tall trees. Climbers and epiphytes seek the supporting structures of tall trees. The woody liane takes hold of those trees at the emergent layer – the Jelutong and the tallest Dipterocarps that assert their space above the canopy.

In the morning, especially following heavy rain, the foliage and mottled trunks glisten infinitely various shades of brown, green, grey and purple, offering the greatest challenge to any artist's palette. The jungle's flowers are mostly inconspicuous, until the Shoreas carpet the forest floor with an abundance of small yellowish or pinkish blossoms that fill the forest with a sweet scent, something like an orange pekoe tea. The Shorea's three-winged fruit, shaped like little shuttlecocks, spin as they fall, and currents of air may carry them long distances.

In the dense tangle of undergrowth, lizards, tree shrews and other woodland creatures scurry through the leaves and up the tree trunks. A spider creates her web in mid-air. Butterflies move silently with us through the still, humid atmosphere. No matter how beckoning the wilder parts might be, it is wise to keep to the established footpaths which will take us through the jungle.

If we leave the jungle by way of Liane Road, we can see where the forest merges with the formally laid-out gardens and have a more comprehensive view of some of the jungle trees retained along the boundary. On our left near the shade rockery stands a Jelutong (*Dyera costulata*), one of the Gardens' giant emergent trees rising above the canopy. Few other Malayan trees can surpass the massive trunk and lofty crown of the forest Jelutong. The interesting shape of the tree and its terminal branching can be more easily observed in a young specimen on Lawn S above the Topiary.

At the corner of Liane and Lower Ring Roads, one venerable old giant, the Jelawei (*Terminalia subspathulata*), stands about 45 metres, or the equivalent of a 15-storey building. Long cords of protective lightning conductors to the top show the Gardens' efforts to preserve this indigenous tree. The Jelawei is identified by its tall, spreading buttresses and conical crown of blunt-tipped leaves shaped like a short spatula. Shrubs of the Trumpet Flower (*Thevetia peruviana*) with yellow and white tubular blossoms and glossy, narrow leaves add a bright, decorative touch at the base. The white latex of this ornamental from tropical America is toxic.

More of the original jungle trees have been retained on Lawn S.

Lower Ring Road

Following the Lower Ring Road eastward with the fringe of forest on our left, we come to a fine example of the Silk-Cotton Tree or Kapok (*Ceiba pentandra*) on Lawn O. The thorny, buttressed trunk unfolds branches at irregular angles. Spirits are said to come and sit on these branches, and it is often found planted near Hindu temples. One of the most common trees in Malayan villages, the Kapok is cultivated throughout tropical Asia and Africa, mainly for the capsules containing a white, woolly fibre used many years commercially to stuff pillows, life jackets, etc. All parts of the tree were used in a variety of medicinal concoctions, including an aphrodisiac in the Philippines. In Singapore, mothers used to soothe nagging coughs with a preparation made of pounded Kapok leaves, an onion and a little turmeric. Just add water and drink three times a day!

Across the Lawn stands a member of the younger generation of the Gardens' trees, the Sandbox-tree (*Hura crepitans*) introduced from tropical America. The fruits of this unusual tree explode with a loud noise when fully ripe to disperse the seeds. The poisonous sap is often used to stupefy fish, and its common name comes from a time when the young fruit served to contain sand used for drying ink, before the invention of blotters.

Returning to the Lower Ring Road and taking the steps downhill toward the potting yard, just outside the gate we find another very tall native tree – prominently buttressed, wearing a thin cloud-cover of leaves, and showing the scars of its age. The Upas-Tree (*Antiaris toxicaria*) is found scattered from southern India to the eastern limits of Malaysia and is most famous for its deadly poison. During the period of tribal wars ranging from China to Indonesia, the poisonous latex was most sought after to coat arrows and darts. Said to remain potent for 48 years in some specimens, the poison arrests the action of the heart and causes convulsions and vomiting once it enters the bloodstream.

The Fernery

Near the entrance to the potting yard, the Gardens' centre of plant propagation, we step down and turn right into a shade rockery dominated by ferns. In the still half-light of this fernery, edged in traffic noises and the throw-away commodities of our complex civilization, are modern representatives of an ancient group of plants that has managed to persist some 400 million years.

Ferns are flowerless, vascular plants that reproduce by spores instead of seeds. Some fern plants root in the ground, some climb high into trees and others – the epiphytic ferns – root and grow on other plants. They are widely distributed over the earth with the greatest and most diverse species concentrated in the humid parts of the tropics, especially in mountain forests. The Malay Peninsula boasts over 500 native fern species, 150 of which may be found in Singapore.

Typical of most true ferns are the young, coiled fronds resembling a shepherd's crook or fiddlehead. Often these are covered with fine hairs or scales. We can observe these distinctive characteristics in two giants of the fern world, the West Indian Tree Fern (*Cyathea arborea*) and the local *Angiopteris evecta*. Species of the latter have thick trunks and enormous leaves, up to 6 metres long under favourable conditions. Delicate Maidenhairs (*Adiantum*), the 'fruit-dotted' *Polypodium*, and a wild assortment of both native and exotic species are also located in the Fernery.

In contrast to the ferns' light leafiness, the Panama Hat-palm (*Carludovica palmata*) waves an imposing clump of three- to five-part fans. Neither a palm, nor a native of Panama, it requires abundant water, good drainage and the same climatic conditions as the ferns. In Equador, the leaves are collected for making 'Panama' hats.

The Plant House and Annex

In the annex to the Plant House, a circular pool displays good examples of epiphytic ferns: the Bird's Nest Fern (*Asplenium nidus*), the Stag's Horn Fern (*Platycerium*), and a fern ally, Clubmoss (*Lycopodium squarrosum*). Given this close range, we can observe the dusty spores on the horn-like fronds of the *Platycerium* and look inside the moist basket of leaf litter from which the fern derives its nutrients. Below, lilies and the tropical aquatic weed with many-flowered lilac-coloured spikes, the Water Hyacinth (*Eichhornia crassipes*), float on the pool's surface.

On the periphery of the annex are beds of *Begonia*, *Calathea* and the insectivorous Pitcher Plant, *Nepenthes* species. The Pitcher Plant's leaf tips are modified to form pitcher-like organs that attract and trap insects. The digestive enzymes in the pitcher drown the insects and then go to work to absorb their nitrogenous food. Three species from Singapore (*Nepenthes rafflesiana*, *N. ampullaria* and *N. gracilis*) represent this novelty in the plant kingdom here.

Since its construction in 1882, the Gardens' Plant House has been the shelter for collections of the more beautiful and ornamental plants. It quickly became the Gardens' showplace with regularly scheduled flower fests and exhibits – and a popular backdrop for wedding portraits.

In the style of English formal gardens, the open courtyard is planned around a central rectangular pool containing Aroids, Papyrus and Cattail reeds. Spade-shaped Junipers and neat hedges summon Alice's vision of a Wonderland garden. We can almost hear the Red Queen shouting, 'Off with her head!'

On the vine-covered arcades are trained the flowering creepers Maiden's Jealousy (*Tristellateia australasica*), Honolulu Creeper (*Antigonon leptopus*), Moon Vine (*Beaumontia multiflora*) from India, and the spectacular Jade Vine (*Strongylodon macrobotrys*) native to the Philippines. In its flowering season, which often coincides with the Chinese New Year (January or February), this vigorous liane bears ½-metre pendulous inflorescences of numerous narrow-winged pea-flowers in jade green. Quite similar to the Jade Vine, the New Guinea Creeper (*Mucuna bennettii*) hangs long trusses of orange-red flowers from the Plant House pergola.

Underneath these climbing vines in the protective semi-shade, the accent is on foliage plants – Aroids, *Dracaenas* and a good selection of Asparagus 'ferns', members of the Lily family that have stems with a fern-like appearance.

Leaving at the midpoint of the Plant House, we climb two flights of bricked steps bordered by pots of gaily coloured annuals.

The Japanese Garden

On Lower Ring Road to our right, against a forest backdrop, a narrow undulating strip of Lawn M has been landscaped in

Top: The old Bandstand, an enduring landmark in the Gardens.
Below: Waterlilies bordering the Plant House.

The Japanese Garden

Two common activities in the Gardens: a student of taiji practising the graceful Chinese art on an early morning, and students collecting specimens beneath an enormous Tembusu (*Fagraea fragrans*).

The Sundial Garden

Sunday afternoon band concert in the Gardens.

One of over 25 varieties of *Plumeria* on Lawn J, the Frangipani Lawn (above).

the style of a Japanese Garden. From Japan, there are shrubby Shore Juniper (*Juniperus conferta*), Snake's Beard grass (*Ophiopogon japonicus*) and the palm-like *Cycas revoluta*. Among the plants selected to suggest those found in Japan's gardens are False Ru (*Baeckia frutescens*), Philippine Pine (*Pinus insularis*) and the Umbrella Plant (*Cyperus flabelliformis*).

Two casually-drawn lily ponds filled with Japanese guppies and carps animate the scene. Boulders, stone lanterns and a simple bamboo fence further enhance the overall effect of quiet, uncluttered space.

Bandstand Hill

From the Japanese Garden looking uphill, we can make out the green octagonal roof of the Bandstand, a conspicuous landmark in the Gardens and little changed since its construction in 1860. When the Gardens were first laid out, a 'band promenade' was to deck the highest point of the Gardens. Here at 33 metres above sea-level, we look out on the circular grassy knoll featuring Singapore's national flower, *Vanda* Miss Joaquim. Tall palms, Junipers and a variety of evergreen and flowering shrubs complete the formal landscape. Children find a playground on the gentle slopes, and in the distance, the scenery changes swiftly from dense vegetation to signs of the City.

As early as the late nineteenth century, this was the site of the Gardens' formal rosary, but all efforts to keep these temperate-climate plants growing at their peak proved futile. Today, after eight years of experimental work with new hybrids, roses are being re-introduced with more hope for success in a covered, hydroponic garden near the Bandstand Hill.

Now heading south we cross Upper Ring Road and duck under the vine-covered pergola. At the foot of the steps on our left, Lawn J has the unmistakeably sweet fragrance and silver gnarled branching of the Frangipani (*Plumeria*). Constantly flowering trees in shades of white to carmine, over 25 varieties may be counted in this grove.

Frangipani is a popular garden, temple and cemetery tree, and the long-lasting blossoms are often made into funeral wreaths or Hawaiian leis worn round the neck. Because of its association with death, the Frangipani will never trim a household vase. Those on the ground you may pick up, sniff the perfume, and tuck behind your ear, as is the custom in these parts. But be careful which ear you choose. A flower worn on the right ear announces to all suitors that you are 'available'.

Several trees of the Leguminosae family share lawn space with the Frangipani collection. A large widespreading Saga (*Adenanthera pavonina*) fills the corner between the slope and Office Ring Road. The Saga can be quite easily identified by the presence of children scrambling round the area on hands and knees searching for 'red stones'. These objects of so much attraction – tiny red seeds – are expelled from the ripened black coiled pods that grow to 20 cm long. The children collect the glossy beads to make necklaces, to use in junket or 'five stones' and other games, or simply for the sake of collecting them. Since antiquity the seeds have also been used as fine weight measures in China and in India's diamond and precious stone trade.

Another common tree in the gardens of India and Sri Lanka, the Golden Shower or Indian Laburnum (*Cassia fistula*), also produces pods that are black when mature, but these are long, pipe-shaped cylinders about 2.5 cm in diameter. Normally the Golden Shower does not flower well in wet climates; in the

Botanic Gardens, however, loose hanging sprays of yellow flowers can cover the entire tree, proving it one of the most beautiful of the yellow Cassias.

The Variegated Coral Tree (*Erythrina variegata*), another long pod producer with brownish seeds, has several distinctive features which make it one of the most colourful in the Gardens. Each leaf is divided into three spade-shaped leaflets, marked by a broad yellow midrib and yellow side veins. The scarlet pea-like flowers are crowded on erect spikes, and their narrow, folded petals are curved in the form of a 'tiger's claw', one of the tree's common names.

The Sundial Garden

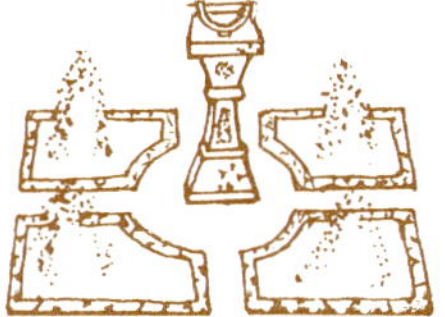

Returning to Lower Ring Road and following the avenue of Sealing Wax Palms uphill, we reach the open, bricked courtyard of the Sundial Garden on Lawn J. Neatly trimmed hedges and beds of ornamental shrubs border four rectangular pools, constructed around a sundial. A floral clock, adding a touch of Switzerland to the tropical setting, adorns the northern slope. The hands of the clock complete their diurnal circle between a smiling lion and Singapore's national banner, the crescent moon with five stars. Jade Vine covered benches providing shady resting places overlook the garden.

Below the Sundial Garden, Lawn J is planted with small collections of Figs and fragrant shrubs and trees. The Indian Rubber (*Ficus elastica*), the Fiddleleaf Fig (*F. lyrata*), the Banyan (*F. benghalensis*), and Spotted Fig (*F. virens*) are here. Krishna's

Cup (*F. krishnae*) holds the centre of attention with far-reaching graceful branches, trimmed in unusual pale green, pocket or cup-shaped leaves and paired figs in bright orange-red with a velvet coat.

This lawn also holds the famous Bo-tree or Bodhi (*Ficus religiosa*), sacred among Buddhists as the tree under which Siddharta Gautama, the Buddha, meditated and attained enlightenment. Spoons are carved from the Fig's wood for sacred uses, and in Burmese and Thai Buddhist temples the clappers of bells are shaped like the flat leaves with characteristic long pointed leaf tips, so that they will ring with the movement of the wind.

Indigenous to Bengal and central India, the Bo-tree was planted as a roadside tree in Singapore during the early days of the Settlement. Because of its religious significance, this 'strangling' epiphyte enjoyed free and prolific growth. Now the species is not encouraged because of the damage it tends to cause house walls and other supporting structures.

The strongly scented Orange Chempaka (*Michelia champaca*) from India stands near Krishna's Cup. It is one of two Chempaka species cultivated for their fragrant flowers in the Malayan region. Malay women choose the showy flowers to adorn their hair, and Indian shops often sell them made up in garlands.

Tiny flowers emitting a strong perfume hang in long racemes from the Fiddlewood (*Citharexylum quadrangulare*). This tropical American tree flowers throughout the year in long, dangling 'earrings' that cover the tree and cast their sweet spell over all of Lawn J.

Another fragrant tree here, *Cratoxylon prunifolium*, native to tropical Asia, flowers in pale pink clusters on mostly leafless branches. The epiphytic Pigeon Orchid (*Dendrobium crumenatum*) has found a nest among the *Cratoxylon* branches. Also a fragrant flower, the orchid's common name comes from its shape which suggests a dove's full breast and curved up-sweep of tail feathers. About seven days following a storm or significant drop in temperature, the orchid opens for a day and then is gone.

The Sun Rockery

Across the road at the northern corner of Lawn E, succulents and other water-storing plants take the full heat of the sun. *Agave* and *Yucca* dominate the collection of very sturdy plants. Brandishing bold, sword-shaped leaves, these New World plants make an interesting contrast to the Old World *Euphorbia*, or 'spurge family' succulents.

Some dramatic shapes are exhibited in the candelabra-formed growth of Dragon Bones (*Euphorbia lactea*) and *E. ingens*, another 'horned' succulent that requires support for its long trunk, and the Milkbush (*E. tirucalli*), a spineless tree with minute leaves and branches clustered irregularly in a crown.

Introduced from Africa over a century and a half ago in this region, 'Tulang-tulang', as the Milkbush is known to the Malays, means 'like bones'. Thus under the assumption that a plant's appearance or 'signature' reflected its curative uses, the boiled stems and roots of the Milkbush were prescribed for painful bones and joints. And the Javanese rubbed the latex 'milk' over bone fractures to insure proper mending.

Scattered below these tall, bony structures, the bushy Crown of Thorns (*Euphorbia milii*) and the Air Plant (*Kalanchoe pinnata*) with long bells drooping in clusters also represent Old World succulents from Madagascar and Africa. Other members of the *Agave* family include the Snake Plant or Mother-in-Law's Tongue (*Sansevieria trifasciata*) and green-striped *Sansevieria cylindrica*. With a few clumps of organ-pipe cactus, we find a good range of the unique shapes that distinguish this tough group of plants.

If you are patient and attentive enough, you might be able to discriminate a chameleon blending with the green tones of its plant perches here. The presence of these creatures in the Sun Rockery calls attention to similarly unique protective mechanisms in cacti and succulents developed over a very long period of time. For as the earth began to dry out and they found themselves in desert land or arid mountain plateaux, these once leafy plants had to simplify their structures to protect themselves and conserve precious water. Thus by developing compact bodies (columnar, globular, pad-shaped), sharp bristles, hooked spines, thick walls, etc., these species managed to survive their changing environment. Today we marvel at the sculptural shapes and textures they evolved essentially as protective devices.

Office Ring Road

Heading south on Office Ring Road, we see a concentration of palms including the Double Coconut on Lawn K. With these well-established trees, a variety of young culinary and fruit trees are planted in an effort to introduce urbanites to important economic plants, now relatively unknown – except as plucked and processed foods from market to table.

The most famous products of the Spice Islands – Clove (*Eugenia aromatica*), Nutmeg (*Myristica fragrans*) and Cinnamon (*Cinnamomum caesia*) – are located here as reminders of the original stock and purpose of the first Botanic Gardens in Singapore. Among the other fruits with yet tender branches are the Australian Macadamia Nut (*Macadamia integrifolia*), the Tamarind (*Tamarindus indicus*) from tropical Asia, Congo Coffee (*Coffea robusta*) from tropical Africa, the Avocado (*Persea americana*) from tropical America and the Curry Bush (*Murraya koenigii*) from the East Indies.

To our right on Lawn E, several intensely colourful *Saracas* exhibit a pale purple shading of new foliage. These young leaf tassels will hang limp for a few days before stiffening and turning green. In March and August the *Saraca* will develop flowers in brilliant bunches, often appearing at the foot of the trunk. On Lawns E and D, you may see examples of the Red Saraca (*Saraca declinata*) from Sumatra, the Malayan Saraca (*S. bijuga*) and the Yellow Saraca (*S. Taipingensis*). Look for these species planted also on Lawns P and Y.

Beyond the *Saracas*, Lawn D contains a collection of Australasian Gymnosperms – Junipers, Araucarias, Podocarps, Pines and Cypresses – resinous, cone-bearing trees of variously shaped leaves. The most striking of these are several scale-leafed Cypresses (*Cupressus*) with very long, outstretched and drooping branches that create an atmosphere of bluish green gloom. Next to them, tall Philippine Pines (*Pinus insularis*) shed prickly needle-like leaves up to 25 cm long. Both Lawns D and B share a good selection of the now familiar Podocarps.

Further around Office Ring Road on our approach to the Office complex, Lawn D has been planted with five species of Butterfly Trees (*Bauhinia*), so named for their twin-lobed leaves in the shape of butterfly wings. These are beautiful, free-flowering trees and shrubs, especially the Hong Kong Bauhinia or Blake's Bauhinia (*Bauhinia blakeana*) which enjoys immense popularity in Singapore's home gardens and parks. The light, wing-leafed branches and showy five-petalled flowers of the White Bauhinia (*B. acuminata*), Purple Bauhinia (*B. purpurea*), *B. reticulata* and *B. racemosa* represent but a few of 150 species known throughout the tropics. These ornamentals and others, such as the yellow variety (*B. tomentosa*), are cultivated elsewhere on the Botanic Gardens' lawns.

Across Office Ring Road on Lawn C stand two well-established examples of the celebrated Para rubber tree (*Hevea brasiliensis*). Near the Office on the same lawn another tall, commanding tree of economic importance to the timber industry has survived to reach the age of 40, in spite of opinions to the contrary when it was planted. The Teak or 'Jati' (*Tectona grandis*) has some distance to grow, however, before it reaches the height of 50 metres achieved by the tallest specimens from the deciduous forests of Burma and Thailand.

Appropriately named after the Greek carpenter 'Tekton', the Teak is world renowned for the hard, heavy, durable wood prized by sculptors, furniture-makers and shipbuilders. Even without its celebrated wood, the beauty of the Teak's quite large, elliptic leaves and full panicles of small white flowers on a rounded crown would assure its position of high esteem in the plant kingdom.

Office, Herbarium and Library

The Botanic Gardens is a Branch of the Parks and Recreation Department under Singapore's Ministry of National Development. Apart from its service as a public park, the Gardens functions as a scientific institution, where research into problems of botanical and horticultural interest is carried out. These buildings house the administrative offices, research laboratories, Herbarium and Library.

The comprehensive Herbarium is stocked with over 600,000 specimens – dried, preserved and mounted on individual sheets. Collected mainly from neighbouring countries, they include specimens that are over 175 years old.

Another important reference centre, the Library holds over 20,000 volumes, including many rare historic texts of the region's flora. These, plus some 500 current journals, prove valuable tools for both academic and applied research of agriculturists, botanists and horticulturists – local and foreign.

In this compound, too, we find the seat of important research work, with emphasis on plant cultivation and propagation, soil testing and plant protection services. This is also the distribution point for orchid plantlets, and trained laboratory assistants enjoy showing visitors how these popular blooms are propagated.

The oldest of the buildings, the single storey with tiled overhanging roof nearest the Office Gate was erected between 1883 and 1892 during Ridley's tenure as Director. Affectionately referred to as 'Ridley's old office', today it serves as a storage area. Directly across the road is located the Park Rangers' office.

Continuing north on Office Ring Road, we pass a small triangular lawn of multi-colourful *Bougainvillea* on our right, and on our left, the collection of palms on Lawn K. These and other now familiar species, such as the venerable old Kapok behind the Rangers' office, are well worth a visit.

Leading us out of the Gardens along Office Gate Road is an avenue of the Caribbee Royal Palm or Cabbage Palm (*Roystonea oleracea*), named for its succulent edible cabbage. From the lowlands of Trinidad and Barbados, this tallest of the Royal

Palm species tapers straight like a column from the enlarged base and shows its grace to full advantage whenever a breeze sways the long branches. Poised like honour-guards on review, the *Roystonea* palms salute us – a fitting farewell to a very special experience.

In the late 1950s, during J.W. Purseglove's tenure as Director of the Gardens, a distinguished visitor was prompted to make this comment in the visitor's book: 'The Singapore Botanic Gardens are unique. Civilization would be the poorer if they were not maintained.'

Perhaps you, too, have found enrichment, a quiet sustenance or simple pleasures here among these new friends you will wish to visit again – discovering in each plant and tree its unique charm and seasonal surprises. And if you come here often enough, you will begin to lay claim to the Botanic Gardens as your own.

Some Suggested Items to make your stroll more pleasurable

1 A canteen of water or fruit juice

2 A hat or lightweight umbrella, preferably cotton, to protect you from the sun

3 Substantial walking shoes for comfort

4 A camera

5 Binoculars

6 A bag to hold plant specimens you may want to gather – but only from the ground!

7 A small waterproof sheet or ground cover

8 A small pad and pencil to record plant names and characteristics, impressions, inspirations, or perhaps the unexpected gift of a poem.

For best results with your camera in the Botanic Gardens:

1 Shoot between 8:30 and 11 a.m. or between 2 and 4:30 p.m. for contrast, crispness and the best quality of light.

2 Use a haze filter.

3 Wear a hat.

4 If you are coming out of an air-conditioned room, allow the camera to warm up about an hour before taking pictures, because humidity condenses on metal and plastic surfaces inside a camera which can cause malfunctions especially in new electronic cameras. So give time for moisture to evaporate out of the camera, or keep it stored in a sealed plastic bag or container.

5 Use fresh film and have it developed soon after your visit to the Botanic Gardens, as film deteriorates rapidly in the tropics.

Glossary

Arboretum	A place grown with trees; a botanic garden of trees.
Aroids	Common name for members of the Araceae family of plants.
Belukar	Secondary jungle, sometimes called *blukar.*
Betel pepper leaves	Leaves of the vine *Piper betle*, grown for chewing. Allied to *Piper nigrum* which yields black pepper.
Corolla	The inner set of a flower's petals, either separate or fused.
Culm	The jointed stem of bamboos and other grasses, usually hollow except at the swollen nodes where leaves are attached.
Emergent tree	A tall tree with its crown above the level of the forest and emerging from its substrate.
Epiphyte	A plant that grows on another plant but does not take nourishment from its host.
Gazebo	An open structure (as a tent, summer house or garden pavilion) designed to command a view.
Inflorescence	A flower cluster, or a floral axis with its appendages.
Lalang	Coarse, tall grasses, sometimes *lallang.*
Lathed	Refers to a roof made of narrow strips of wood set apart so as to allow light to filter through.
Liane, liana	A woody, climbing plant that roots in the ground and is characteristic of tropical rain forests.
Mescal	A Mexican liquor distilled from the central leaves of the Maguey or Century Plant (*Agave americana*) after being roasted and fermented.
Monocotyledon	A seed plant that produces an embryo with a single seed-leaf.
Obconic	More or less conical, with the apex below or forming the point of attachment.

Orange pekoe	Refers to Indian or Ceylonese tea flavoured with orange.
Palmate	Having the shape of a hand with fingers spread.
Pericarp	The wall of a ripened ovary (fruit).
Petiole	A slender stem that supports the blade of a foliage leaf; a leafstalk.
Pinnate	Resembling a feather, especially in having similar parts arranged on opposite sides of an axis.
Raceme	An inflorescence in which flowers are borne on stalks of about equal length along an elongated axis that continues to grow during flowering.
Spathe	A bract or leaf surrounding a flower cluster or a fleshy flower spike.
Spike	A long, unbranched inflorescence set with stalkless flowers.
Spurge family	Plants of the family Euphorbiaceae (especially the genus *Euphorbia*).
Temenggong	The highest ranking official in a Malay village.
Tequila	A Mexican liquor made by redistilling mescal.
Terminal panicle	Pyramid-shaped, loosely branched flower cluster borne at the end of a twig.

Chronology of Important Historical Events

1819	First spice plants are introduced on Government Hill.
1822–23	First Botanic Gardens in Singapore is laid out on Government Hill.
1829	First Gardens is discontinued and the land parcelled out.
1836–46	An Agri-Horticultural Society resurrects a small 2.8 hectare plot from the original tract.
1859	A new Singapore Agri-Horticultural Society establishes the Botanic Gardens at the Tanglin site.
1859–75	Nutmeg planter Lawrence Niven supervises the layout of the Gardens.
1866	Construction begins on the Superintendent's House, now the location of the School of Ornamental Horticulture.
1874	The Gardens is given over to government administration and formally opened to the public.
1875–80	James Murton, a Kew-trained horticulturist, supervises the Gardens.
1877	Para rubber (*Hevea brasiliensis*) seedlings arrive from Kew Gardens and are planted in the Palm Valley.
1879	Economic Gardens is established on the 41 hectare tract northeast of the Botanic Gardens.
1880–88	Nathaniel Cantley is Superintendent of the Gardens.
1880	Cantley formally establishes the Herbarium.
1882	Plant House is constructed.
1883	Construction begins on 'Ridley's old office', the one-storey bungalow nearest the Office Gate.
1888–1912	H.N. Ridley is Director of the Gardens.
1891	Ridley begins publication of the *Agricultural Bulletin*, the first in a near-continuous series of scientific journals sponsored by the Gardens.

1893	Agnes Joaquim discovers the natural orchid hybrid that will bear her name and become Singapore's national flower.
1896	Tan Chay Yan plants the first trial crop of Para rubber.
1903	The first level of the Herbarium is constructed. Level two is added in 1930.
1912–25	I.H. Burkill is Director of the Gardens.
1924	Economic Gardens is discontinued with construction of Raffles College.
1926–49	Eric Holttum is Director of the Gardens.
1928	Holttum begins artificial orchid hybridization in the Botanic Gardens.
1929–45	E.J.H. Corner is Assistant Director of the Gardens.
1942–46	Kwan Koriba is Director of the Gardens during the Japanese occupation of Singapore.
1949–54	M.R. Henderson is Director of the Gardens.
1954–57	J.W. Purseglove is Director of the Gardens.
1957–69	H.M. Burkill is Director of the Gardens.
1963	Prime Minister Lee Kuan Yew launches the 'Garden City' campaign, in which the majority of the trees, or some 6000 saplings, are supplied by the Gardens.
1970	Chew Wee Lek is Director of the Gardens.
1970–76	A.G. Alphonso is Acting Director of the Gardens.
1972	Classes begin at the School of Ornamental Horticulture.
1973	Botanic Gardens becomes a branch of the Parks and Recreation Division, now a Department under the Ministry of National Development.
1976–	Mrs Ng Siew Yin is Assistant Commissioner of Parks and Recreation, Botanic Gardens Branch.

List of Major References Consulted

Abdullah bin Abdul Kadir, *The Hikayat Abdullah; An Annotated Translation by A.H. Hill.* Singapore, 1955.

Allen, Betty Molesworth, *Some Common Trees of Malaysia and Singapore*. Singapore, 1971.

Annual Reports, Botanic Gardens. Singapore, beginning 1879.

Annual Reports, Ministry of National Development. Singapore, 1975–82.

Bailey, Liberty Hyde and Ethel Zoe Bailey, comps., *Hortus Third: A Concise Dictionary of Plants Cultivated in the United States and Canada*. New York, 1976. (Revised and expanded version.)

Bastin, John, ed., 'The Letters of Sir Stamford Raffles to Nathaniel Wallich 1819–1824', *Journal of the Malaysian Branch of the Royal Asiatic Society*, LIV, pt. 2 (December 1981), 1–73.

Buckley, Charles Burton, *An Anecdotal History of Old Times in Singapore*. Kuala Lumpur, 1965.

Burkill, I.H., *The Botanic Gardens Singapore, Illustrated Guide*. Singapore, 1926.

_____, *A Dictionary of the Economic Products of the Malay Peninsula*. 2 vols. Kuala Lumpur, 1966.

Corner, E.J.H. and K. Watanabe, *Illustrated Guide to Tropical Plants*. Tokyo, 1969.

Corner, E.J.H., *The Marquis: A Tale of Syonan-to*. Singapore, 1981.

_____, *Wayside Trees of Malaya*. 2 vols. Singapore, 1952.

The Gardens' Bulletin, Singapore. Singapore, 1947–82.

The Gardens' Bulletin, Straits Settlements. Singapore, 1913–41.

A Guide to Tree Planting. Singapore, 1981. (Parks and Recreation Department, Ministry of National Development.)

Hooi, Christopher, 'First Successful Planting of the Rubber Tree Hevea brasiliensis in the Botanic Gardens, Singapore', *Heritage*, No. 2 (1977), 21–30.

Makepeace, Walter, Gilbert E. Brooke and Roland St. J. Braddell, eds., *One Hundred Years of Singapore*. London, 1921.

A Pictorial Guide to the Singapore Botanic Gardens. Singapore, 1974.

Selected Plants and Planting for a Garden City: forty popular climbers. Singapore (1975).

Selected Plants and Planting for a Garden City: forty shrubs. Singapore (1975).

Selected Plants and Planting for a greener Singapore. Singapore (1976).

Teoh Eng Soon, *A Joy Forever*. Singapore, 1982.

Turnbull, C.M., *A History of Singapore 1819–1975*. Kuala Lumpur, 1977.

Whitmore, T.C., *Palms of Malaya*. Kuala Lumpur, 1973.

Wurtzburg, C.E., *Raffles of the Eastern Isles*. London, 1954.

Index to Botanical Names

Index to Common Names